AN INTRODUCTION TO THE BIBLE

VOLUME ONE
BIBLE
SURVEY SERIES

an Introduction to the Bible

L. D. JOHNSON

Convention
Press
Nashville,
Tennessee

This book is the text for a course in the subject area Bible Studies of the Church Study Course.

Target group: This book is designed for adults and is part of the Church Study Course offerings. The 1963 statement of "The Baptist Faith and Message" is the doctrinal guideline for the writer and editor.

Dewey Decimal Classification Number: 220
Printed in the United States of America

Contents

To
CAROLE
1939–1963

Let not my mind be blinder by more light
Nor faith, by reason added, lose her sight.

—JOHN DONNE

Preface

"This [book] is written to tell what kind of book the Bible is, how it came together, what its unifying themes are, and what it says to us today. Hopefully along the way there will emerge a deeper appreciation for and a firmer confidence in the Bible as the Word of God. Information should not be a hindrance but a help to genuine faith."

These words, which appear in the opening paragraphs of this book, sum up the purpose and content of L. D. Johnson's work. In fact, they are an adequate summary of the purpose of the Bible Survey series.

AN INTRODUCTION TO THE BIBLE is volume 1 of an eight-volume set published by Convention Press. These books are designed as part of the new Church Study Course. They are meant to be used as a part of an intensive Bible Survey course in a church, in a mission, in a home, on a college campus, in private—in any setting where the Bible can and should be studied.

In this book, Dr. Johnson discusses the Bible as a covenant in two parts, as one book and many books; and he gives attention to the Bible in relationship to history, science, and literature. Chapter 2, "How God Is Related to the Bible," is an eloquent and moving presentation of the Bible as the revelation of God to man. The Bible gains deeper significance for us as we ponder these words: "The Bible is both an announcement of something that happened and also a stirring witness to each one who gets involved in the message. The liberation did not happen just 'once upon a time,' but it continues to happen wherever the Bible is faithfully preached and heard in repentance and faith."

AN INTRODUCTION TO THE BIBLE should lay a firm foundation for the seven other volumes in the series. (See back cover for titles and authors.)

Mavis Allen, Editor

L. D. Johnson, born in Walters, Oklahoma, is chaplain and professor of religion at Furman University in Greenville, South Carolina. Dr. Johnson received his early education in the public schools of Walters. He was graduated in 1937 from George Washington University with an A.B. degree. He received the Masters degree in theology from Southern Baptist Theological Seminary in 1940 and the Doctor of Theology degree from the same institution in 1942.

The Church Study Course

The Church Study Course consists of a variety of short-term credit courses for adults and youth and noncredit foundational units for children and preschoolers. The materials are for use in addition to the study and training curriculums made available to the churches on an ongoing basis.

Study courses and foundational units are organized into a system that is promoted by the Sunday School Board, 127 Ninth Avenue, North, Nashville, Tennessee 37234; by the Woman's Missionary Union, 600 North Twentieth Street, Birmingham, Alabama 35203; by the Brotherhood Commission, 1548 Poplar Avenue, Memphis, Tennessee 38104; and by the respective departments of the state conventions affiliated with the Southern Baptist Convention.

Study course materials are flexibile enough to be adapted to the needs of any Baptist church. The resources are published in several different formats—textbooks of various sizes, workbooks, and kits. Each item contains a brief explanation of the Church Study Course and information on requesting credit. Additional information and interpretation are available from the participating agencies.

Types of Study and Credit

Adults and youth can earn study course credit through individual or group study. Teachers of courses or of foundational units also are eligible to receive credit.

1. Class Experience.—Group involvement with course material for the designated number of hours for the particular course. A person who is absent from one or more sessions must complete the "Personal Learning Activities" or other requirements for the material missed.

2. Individual Study.—This includes reading, viewing, or listening to course material and completing the specified requirements for the course.

3. Lesson Course Study.—Parallel use of designated study course material during the study of selected units in Church Program Organization periodical curriculum units. Guidance for this means of credit appears in the selected periodical.

4. Institutional Study.—Parallel use of designated study course material during regular courses at educational institutions, including Seminary Extension Department courses. Guidance for this means of credit is provided by the teacher.

Credit is awarded for the successful completion of a course of study. This credit is granted by the Church Study Course Awards Office, 127 Ninth Avenue, North, Nashville, Tennessee 37234, for the participating agencies. Form 151 (available free) is recommended for use in requesting credit.

When credit is issued to a person on request, the Awards Office sends two copies of a notice of credit earned to the church. The original copy of the credit slip should be filed by the study course clerk in the participant's record of training folder. The duplicate should be given to the person who earned the credit. Accumulated credits are applied toward leadership or member development diplomas, which are measures of learning, growth, development, and training.

Detailed information about the Church Study Course system of credits, diplomas, and record keeping is available from the participating agencies. Study course materials, supplementary teaching or learning aids, and forms for record keeping may be ordered from Baptist Book Stores.

The Church Study Course Curriculum

Credit is granted on those courses listed in the current copy of *Church Services and Materials Catalog, Church Study Course Catalog,* and *Baptist Book Store Catalog.* When selecting courses or foundational units, check the current catalogs to determine what study course materials are valid.

How to Request Credit for This Course

This book is the text for a course in the subject area Bible Studies.

This course is designed for 10 hours of group study. Credit is awarded for satisfactory class experience with the study material for the minimum number of hours. A person who is absent from one or more sessions must complete the "Personal Learning Activities" or other requirements for the materials missed.

Credit is also allowed for use of this material in individual study and in institutional study, if so designated.

The following requirements must be met for credit in this course:

1. Read the book *An Introduction to the Bible.*
2. Attend at least 10 hours of class study or complete all "Personal Learning Activities" (pp. 148-50). A class member who is absent from one or more class sessions must complete "Personal Learning Activities" on chapters missed. In such a case, he must turn in his paper by the date the teacher sets, usually within ten days following the last class.

Credit in this course may be earned through individual study. The requirements for such credit are:

1. Read the book.
2. Complete the "Personal Learning Activities" on the chapters.

Credit in this course may be earned through study in an educational institution, if so designated by a teacher. The requirements are:

1. Read the book.
2. Fulfill the requirements of the course taught at the institution.

After the course is completed, the teacher, the study course records librarian, the learner, or any person designated by the church should complete Form 151 ("Request for Course Credit") and send it to the Awards Office, 127 Ninth Avenue, North, Nashville, Tennessee 37234. In the back of this book the reader will find a form which he may cut out, fill in, and send to the Awards Office.

Bibliography *

Cartledge, Samuel A. *The Bible: God's Word to Man.* Nashville: Broadman Press, 1967.*

Conner, Walter Thomas. *The Faith of the New Testament.* Nashville: Broadman Press, 1940.

Criswell, Wallie A. *The Bible for Today's World.* Grand Rapids: Zondervan Publishing House, 1965.

Criswell, Wallie A. *Why I Preach That the Bible Is Literally True.* Nashville: Broadman Press, 1969.

Dana, Harvey Eugene, and Glaze, R. E., Jr. *Interpreting the New Testament.* Nashville: Broadman Press, 1961.

Farb, Peter. *The Land, Wildlife, and Peoples of the Bible.* New York: Harper & Row, 1967.

Gift, Joseph L. *Life and Customs in Jesus' Time.* Cincinnati: Standard Publishing, 1957.

Keller, Werner. *The Bible as History: A Confirmation of the Book of Books.* New York: William Morrow & Company, 1956.

Lightfoot, Neil R. *How We Got the Bible.* Grand Rapids: Baker Book House, 1963.

---

* The listing of these books does not imply endorsement of their total contents by author or publishers of AN INTRODUCTION TO THE BIBLE.

MacGregor, Geddes. *A Literary History of the Bible; From the Middle Ages to the Present Day*. Nashville: Abingdon Press, 1968.

Monsma, John C. *The Evidence of God in an Expanding Universe*. New York: G. P. Putnam's Sons, 1958.

Newman, Barclay Moon. *The Meaning of the New Testament*. Nashville: Broadman Press, 1966.

Pfeiffer, Charles F. (ed.). *The Biblical World: A Dictionary of Biblical Archaeology*. Grand Rapids: Baker Book House, 1966.

Pfeiffer, Charles F., and Vos, Howard F. *The Wycliffe Historical Geography of Bible Lands*. Chicago: Moody Press, 1967.

Reid, James. *God, the Atom and the Universe*. Grand Rapids: Zondervan Publishing House, 1968.

Tenney, Merrill Chapin. *New Testament Times*. Grand Rapids: William B. Eerdmans Publishing Company, 1965.

Tidwell, Josiah Blake. *The Bible Period by Period*. Nashville: Broadman Press, 1941.

Vardaman, E. Jerry. *Archaeology and the Living Word*. Nashville: Broadman Press, 1965.

Watts, James Washington. *Old Testament Teaching*. Nashville: Broadman Press, 1967.

Wegener, Gunther S. *6000 Years of the Bible*. New York: Harper & Row, 1963.

CHAPTER ONE

What Kind
of Book
Is the Bible?

For church people it would appear unnecessary to write an introduction to the Bible. Have we not been studying the Bible in Sunday School all our lives? Do we not regularly hear it extolled and its teachings explained from our pulpits? Is it not the pillar of cloud by day and the pillar of fire by night of our faith?

All of this is true—or at least partially so. But there is reason to believe that we praise the Bible a good deal more than we study it. Misinformation about the Bible and ignorance of its nature and teachings are more the rule than the exception. Many who faithfully avow that the Bible supplies God's answer to every human problem would be hard put to tell where or how the answers may be found. Tests of students beginning college courses in Bible have consistently shown up the depressingly poor job of Bible teaching we have been doing in the churches.

If church people do not know much about the Bible, one may be certain that the growing masses of the unchurched know and care less. Statistics assure us that the Bible is still the world's best seller, but evidence of biblical literacy is not encouraging. The late Bruce Barton was too painfully near the truth when he entitled his book about the Bible *The Book Nobody Knows*.

This book is written not simply to praise the Bible, although the writer stands in the mainstream of Baptist conviction that the Bible is the unique and divinely-inspired record of God's redemptive revelation of himself. The task is not undertaken to inspire and urge study of the Bible, although it is devoutly hoped that the book might have that effect. This is written to tell what kind of book the Bible is, how it came together, what its unifying themes are, and what it says to us today. Hopefully along the way there will emerge a deeper appreciation for and a firmer confidence in the Bible as the Word of God. Information should not be a hindrance but a help to genuine faith.

The Covenant in Two Parts

If you were to open a Bible for the first time, the thing that might immediately attract your attention is that there are two major divisions in it: "Old Testament" and "New Testament." If you have been exposed to the Bible all your life, you know that the first and longer division concerns events and personalities through which God was working prior to the time of Christ. The second part of the Bible deals with the events surrounding the life of Christ and the subsequent beginnings and early experience of the church.

If you were Jewish, you would likely view the first part of this literature as divinely inspired, but not the second. Inasmuch as you are a Christian, you believe that the second fulfils what was promised in the first and that the two together comprise "the true center of Christian union, and the supreme standard by which all human conduct, creeds, and religious opinions should be tried." [1] The first part without the second is incomplete.

Perhaps the reason for this relationship will be clearer when the word "testament" is clarified. A better English translation of the biblical word would be "covenant." We have an "old covenant" and a "new covenant" in the Bible. The covenant concept is pivotal in our understanding of the Bible. It is the basis of the relationship between God and Israel and between God and the "new Israel," the church. To understand the message and continuity of the Scriptures, it is necessary to see the centrality of the covenant as the basis of God's relationship with his people.

"Covenant" means an agreement made between two parties, in this case between God and his people. One unique feature of the biblical covenant, however, is that it is not an agreement or contract reached between two equals after bargaining. The holy God rightly demands obedience, promising his blessing of redemption to those who are faithful to the obligations of the covenant. "Now therefore, if you will obey my voice and keep my covenant, you shall be my own possession among all peoples; for all the earth is mine, and you shall be to me a kingdom of priests and a holy nation" (Ex. 19:5–6, RSV).

In many places and circumstances the covenant is expressed in the Old Testament. From the story of the fall of man in the Garden of Eden there comes the first expression of the covenant hope. In what is often termed the *protoevangelium,* a foretaste of the gospel, the promise is made that the seed of woman shall bruise the head of the serpent. The promise symbolized by the rainbow after the flood in the days of Noah is seen as another expression of the covenant (Gen. 9:8–17).

Abraham also received the promise and responded by going out, "not knowing whither he went" (Heb. 11:8), from Mesopotamia, the land of his forefathers, to Canaan (Palestine), the land which God promised to give to him and his descendants. This great man is pictured in Genesis as the figure who epitomized the covenant relationship between God and his chosen people in the patriarchal days. The outward symbol of the covenant relationship from the time of Abraham onward was the mark of circumcision (Gen. 17).

Again the covenant was renewed and made more explicit at Sinai under the leadership of Moses. The essence of the covenant was embodied in the Ten Commandments. (See Ex. 20; 34; Deut. 5.) Here are expressed the terms of agreement offered by a holy God to his chosen people. It is a covenant based upon what God has done, demanding holy obedience in return. Four of the Ten Commandments clarify specific obligations of the covenanter toward God, while the last six relate to man's responsibility toward his fellowman. Thus, the covenant has dimensions of both obedience to God and service to others. The Ten Commandments are an expression of the covenant in the form of certain great principles. They may be thought of as the giant beams which support a building.

Each generation was called upon to renew the covenant for itself. For example, such a renewal is reported in Joshua 24 following the conquest of Canaan by Israel. Another striking occasion of covenant renewal came in 621 B.C. when King Josiah of Judah called his people to national repentance and rededication after a scroll containing the law had been discovered by workmen repairing the Temple (2 Kings 22–23).

After King David, the covenant was linked with him and his descendants in Judah. It was the same covenant that had been binding upon Israel from the beginning, but now it was identified with the promise of an unbroken succession through the Davidic line. When the Davidic line ended with the capture of Jerusalem in 589 B.C. and the exile in Babylon, it became necessary to reevaluate the meaning of the covenant. Some spoke of a restoration of the Davidic dynasty at a future date. Others began to interpret the covenant promise as a spiritual and internal one.

Such an interpreter was the prophet Jeremiah, who came near the end of Judah's national history before the exile to Babylon. With prophetic vision of the relationship which God wants with his people, Jeremiah described the "new covenant." It was to be an inner, spiritual bond between God and his people, written "upon their hearts" (Jer. 31:33, RSV).

Christians understand this covenant promise to have been fulfilled in the events recorded in the Gospels. Christ came and established the new covenant by his life, death, and resurrection. He is the fulfilment of all that had been promised. Moreover, his coming is seen as explicitly establishing a "new Israel" composed of all who by repentance and faith accept the relationship which God the Father has offered through his Son, Jesus Christ. As Jesus sat in the upper room at the Last Supper, he took a cup and gave thanks, and said: "Drink ye all of it; for this is my blood of the new testament [covenant], which is shed for many for the remission of sins" (Matt. 26:27–28).

We are people of the covenant. The Bible is the record of the covenant relationship with God. It is a covenant perfectly fulfilled and expressed in Jesus Christ. The old covenant has not been replaced by the covenant of grace, but it has been fulfilled. All that was expressed in the old covenant is embodied in the new. But more than that, the old covenant finds its highest meaning in the new covenant of Christ. When you open your Bible and see the two divisions of Old and New Testaments, remember that the terms are not meaningless designations of two parts of the Bible. Rather, they represent a major theme of the biblical revelation.

One Book and Many Books

After noting that it has two major divisions or volumes, which the knowledgeable reader sees as Parts 1 and 2 of the same revelation, the newcomer to the Bible might observe that it has numerous subdivisions. It is unlike an ordinary book which tells a continuing story from beginning to end, for there is often little discernible connection between the subdivisions.

On the other hand, it cannot be termed an anthology for it is unlike a collection of writings by various authors. Many of the subdivisions tell the same story, as, for example, the four Gospels in the New Testament and the Kings and Chronicles accounts of the monarchies of Judah and Israel in the Old Testament. Not only are there such repetitions in subject matter (although each "book" is singular in representing its own peculiar viewpoint of the events reported), but there are cases of exact duplication of material. Examples of this are found in Isaiah 2:2–4 and Micah 4:1–3, and in Jeremiah 52 and 2 Kings 24:18 to 25:30.

The Protestant accepts sixty-six of these subdivisions as comprising his Bible, thirty-nine in the Old Testament and twenty-seven in the New. Roman Catholics admit to their Old Testament fourteen in addition to the thirty-nine. These were included in the Greek translation of the Old Testament which was done by Jews in Alexandria, Egypt, in the third and second centuries B.C. Since these "extra" books were never included in the Hebrew Bible, which is the language of the Old Testament, Protestants consider them to be outside the confines of sacred Scripture and call them "The Apocrypha." This term comes from a Greek word meaning "hidden," and suggests that their origin is unknown and the material untrustworthy as Scripture.

It is properly called "Bible," for the word is derived from a Greek word meaning book or booklets. The word "holy" means "separate," "set apart," and suggests the conviction of believers through the centuries that the Holy Bible is uniquely sacred.

This collection of writings covers many centuries. The first eleven chapters of Genesis reflect upon that long indeterminate period from creation to the time of Abraham. From Abraham to the close of the New Testament era is a span roughly equal to the time between the birth of Christ and now. It is obvious, therefore, that the material in the books of the Bible is highly selective. What was included and what was omitted reveal the divine purpose to record and preserve the account of God's redemptive activity in and through Israel for the whole human race.

Further, these sixty-six books mirror the experience of a wide variety of people at various stages of their development and spiritual understanding. Countless unknown contributors added their bit to the record of God's dealings with Israel. It needs to be said plainly that the books are of unequal spiritual vision. For example, however we may seek to justify and explain the rather terrifying records of the conquest of Canaan in the book of Joshua, they cannot be favorably compared to the moral grandeur of the Sermon on the Mount. Nor can all of the psalms be read as equally helpful. How could one equate Psalm 23, for example, with Psalm 69, a prayer against one's enemies? Then there is Psalm 109 in which the writer prays for the death of his enemy, that his enemy's parents may never have their sins forgiven, and that his children may be beggars with no one to pity them.

We need feel no lack of loyalty to or love of the Bible because we acknowledge that some passages do not come up to the standards of Christ. Would it not be strange if the spiritual understanding of Joshua, 1,250 years before Christ, were equal to that of our Lord himself? God did not change in the intervening centuries, but man's understanding of the revelation of him did—even inspired man's understanding changed.

The Bible did not "fall from heaven" complete from beginning to end. To believe such a thing may be good Moslem doctrine, or good Mormon doctrine, for both of these religions teach that their sacred books, the Koran and the Book of Mormon respectively, were given as finished products. But it is not good Christian doctrine, for we know that the Bible was gradually brought together over the course of many centuries under God's direction. It was the work of countless people whose understanding of the revelation they were given was colored by the times in which they lived, but which depended more on God's knowledge.

Another aspect of the Bible's nature which is noticeable from the most casual examination is that it is not a straight narrative of events from creation to the end of the New Testament era. Later chapters (pp. 31–98) in this book will give a brief review of the material in both of the Testaments, but let us note here that there are numerous types of writing in the Bible in addition to the narrative. There is a collection of poems or songs which were used in worship. These are found in the book of Psalms. There are other collections of oracles, prophecies, or sermons. These are found in the books which bear the names of the men who were identified with the prophecies, such as Isaiah, Amos, Jeremiah, and Micah. There are collections of "wisdom sayings," pithy observations on life and its foibles and grandeur. Examples are the book of Proverbs, Ecclesiastes, and Job. There are lengthy passages recording detailed ritual and legal matters, such as appear in Leviticus.

When one turns to the New Testament, the same kind of diversity in types of material is found. There are first of all the four Gospels, reporting not only selected incidents and sayings from the life of Christ but also the early church's understanding of him. These were written after the gospel had spread across the Roman Empire and subsequent to the establishment of many churches and the appearance of the letters of the apostle Paul. Then there is Acts, which is largely a record of the work of the Holy Spirit through the early Christian community. A series of letters by Paul and others is included, some of which are addressed to individuals, some to churches, and others to believers in general, and all of which serve as commentaries upon the gospel and the manner in which it is being received. Lastly, there is the Revelation, full of symbolic promise of the ultimate victory of Christ over the world.

From this brief exercise of thumbing through the Bible, it is clear why people who do not know what they are looking for may become confused and give up in despair of being able to understand. This is not to say that the sincere and conscientious seeker cannot find salvation by reading the Bible without guidance. It is to point out the plain truth, however, that the Bible's inexhaustible store of truth becomes more meaningful when we know something of the nature of the Scriptures we are reading. The Ethiopian eunuch's reply to Philip's inquiry as to whether he understood what he was reading from the book of Isaiah is instructive here. He answered, " 'How can I, unless some one guides me? ' " (Acts 8:31, RSV).

The Bible and History

The Bible is primarily an action book. This is to say, it is not an elaboration of theories on the qualities of the good life, speculation concerning the existence and character of the Supreme Being, or philosophical studies on the nature of man. It is, rather, a record of events through which God has acted on behalf of all men. The Bible is the record of selective events in which God is seen as acting for the sake of man's redemption.

An important key to our understanding of the Bible is the phrase "selective event." The Christian faith understands itself to be a religion of revelation; that is, God has unveiled himself. God has done this so that man, whose vision of God and of his own nature has been disastrously distorted by his sin, may see. Seeing God's nature and purpose and seeing himself in his sinfulness, man may be moved to repentance and trust in God's redemptive work.

But this "unveiling" is not done through messages—press releases handed down from heaven concerning the state of celestial affairs and having no particular relationship to anything occurring in the world. Rather, it is done through events that involve people. History is the arena in which revelation has occurred. God has communicated himself in and through what happened. It was, in fact, God who was acting upon the stage of human history, acting always in such a way as to instruct his people of the covenant and encourage them to accept and fulfil their mission as his redemptive agents to all the human family.

Thus the Bible, a record of God in action through his people, looks upon history with the eye of faith. This means that it reports historical events as being related to the divine purpose. It is not non-historical, but it is history from a particular perspective—the meaning of God's creative work, the disruption caused by man's sin, and God's continuing and loving redemptive action.

Moreover, the Bible is selective in the reporting of events. One should not read it for a survey of ancient history. It is by no means such a document. Rather, it is the focusing on a small—and to the world, insignificant—people to show what God has done for all mankind. It is as if a divine telephoto lens has been used to pick out one individual in a huge crowd and zoom in on him to give a close-up of his life. It was not as if the biblical writers knew nothing of the great happenings of their world, although they may indeed have been largely unaware of such movements. It was, rather, that they wrote from a specific motivation—a divine urging to tell how God had revealed his purpose through a Chosen People.

For example, turn back to Genesis 11–12 and trace the biblical account of the westward trek of Abraham from Ur of the Chaldees, and later from Haran in Upper Mesopotamia, to Canaan. From an historical and sociological viewpoint, this was doubtless merely an instance in the centuries-long migration of numberless, nameless clans of Semitic desert nomads into the Fertile Crescent. Great migrations of Amorites, Semitic forebears of Israel, came into Canaan in the first part of the second millennium B.C. From the standpoint of biblical revelation, the importance of this event lay in the fact that God chose Abraham, a man of faith, to be the bearer of the covenant and the father of Israel.

Or, review the chapters in Genesis which tell of the descent of Joseph to Egypt through the cruelty of his brothers, his subsequent rise to power, and the eventual coming of all of Joseph's family from Canaan to the Land of the Nile. Examination of Egyptian history shows that this vignette of Hebrew family life had as its background the period of the domination of Egypt by a powerful Semitic people called Hyksos from the eighteenth to the sixteenth centuries B.C. With the use of advanced weapons such as the chariot and the laminated bow, these invaders overturned the native Egyptian dynasty about 1710 B.C. and established a strong government in the Nile Delta. For a century and a half they controlled Egypt and Canaan. This was the period of Joseph and his family, and, although the biblical narrative is confined to the affairs of this one family, the broader background into which their story was set is that outlined above. During the Hyksos period, then, when Egypt was under Semitic rule, Joseph came to power. But from the Bible's view the remarkable career of Joseph, enabling him to save not only his own family but Egypt as well, was a clear illustration of the way God was leading his people.

In time there arose a pharaoh "who knew not Joseph," and the people of Israel were enslaved and subjected to humiliating treatment. Historically, the Hyksos were expelled from Egypt in 1570 B.C., and a new and vigorous native Egyptian dynasty rose to power. The Nile Delta capital of the Hyksos (Avaris) was destroyed, and the capital returned to its ancient site in Upper Egypt, Thebes. The descendants of Joseph occupied the Delta, formerly the seat of government. After the restoration of a native Egyptian dynasty, these "foreigners" were enslaved.

Against such a historical backdrop the Exodus takes place. Seen by the Old Testament as the pivotal event—the moment of liberation—the Exodus is nowhere mentioned in Egyptian records. There is good evidence that it occurred during the reign of Rameses II, one of the foremost of Egypt's kings. While he might have chosen to obliterate any record of the deliverance of the Hebrew slaves from his land, the fact is that the event happened in a particular historical setting and that the biblical writers viewed it as crucial.

Thus, what might have appeared to others as insignificant was often seen by Israel as a primary example of God's participation in her life. Contrariwise, what the world saw as important might be barely mentioned or totally obscured in the biblical record because it contributed little or nothing to the story of God working out his purpose through Israel.

A classic example of this exclusion of historical material by the biblical writers is the handling of the career of King Omri. This man founded a strong dynasty in Israel in the ninth century B.C., established Samaria as his capital, and brought stability and prosperity to his country. Evidently his neighbors were impressed. A famous Moabite archaeological find records Omri's subjugation of the Moabites, and an Assyrian inscription dated one hundred and fifty years after Omri still refers to Israel as "the land of Omri." Yet the book of Kings in the Bible accorded him only thirteen verses while devoting six chapters to his son Ahab, a much less important figure from the historical perspective. The reason for this is quite clear. King Ahab and his infamous Canaanite queen, Jezebel, were principals in that pivotal struggle between the immoral fertility cult, Baalism, and Yahwism, the faith of Israel and the great prophet, Elijah.

The same theological interpretation of history which has been noted in the Old Testament may be seen also in the New. To be sure, the historical accuracy of the New Testament claims concerning Jesus Christ and the early church may be confidently trusted by the Christian. After all, the first New Testament writings concerning Christ and his work (e.g., 1 Cor.) began to appear no more than a quarter of a century after the events themselves. And by the time Luke wrote his Gospel (possibly forty or more years after the events), he began by reporting that "many have undertaken to compile a narrative of the things which have been accomplished among us" (Luke 1:1, RSV). That the New Testament has its setting in historical events and is about people "with names and addresses" is scarcely open to serious doubt.

Yet the New Testament is itself composed of interpretations of events as well as simple reports of events. All of the Gospels ignore the long years of Jesus' growing up in Nazareth, for instance. Other than Luke's inclusion of the incident of his visit to the Temple at Jerusalem when he was twelve, we know nothing of him from infancy until he was thirty. Further, all of the Gospels devote a disproportionate amount of their material (Mark approximately one half) to the closing weeks of his ministry. It is obvious that we do not have a balanced biography of Jesus in these Gospels, but a selection of material chosen under the guidance of the Holy Spirit to witness to Christ. John put this matter of the selective use of events plainly when he wrote near the end of his Gospel: "Now Jesus did many other signs in the presence of the disciples, which are not written in this book; but these are written that you may believe that Jesus is the Christ, the Son of God, and that believing you may have life in his name" (20:30–31, RSV).

In summary, then, it can be said that the Bible is set in history. The matters it relates have to do with a particular people in particular times and places. However, it is obvious that it includes material which is parabolic and symbolic; and the reader needs to be aware of this fact and not be embarrassed by it or fearful that the validity of the Scriptures is threatened. More will appear about this in the section "The Bible as Literature" at the end of this chapter.

It is not accurate to say only that the Bible is history, for it is history with a special purpose. It is history as seen from the perspective of commitment that God is at work in and through his people for the redemption of all who have faith in his Son, Jesus Christ. Not only is the Bible written from this viewpoint; but, as we have seen, it is selective writing. It is writing which emphasizes those experiences and events which describe and illustrate God's saving work and gives little or no notice to other experiences and events which do not.

The Bible and Science

The observation that the Bible is not a book of science is often misunderstood. Those who are inclined to exalt the scientific and technological method are apt to suppose that the statement is an admission of the Bible's inferiority as a source of authority and truth.

Those defensive about the Bible sometimes mistake the statement as an attack on the Bible's reliability. Neither conclusion is warranted.

The simple fact is that the Bible was not written in a scientific age nor was it written by men inspired by the scientific method or equipped with scientific data. The method of science is inductive; for example, the scientist gathers evidence which points to a certain conclusion. He tests it and experiments with it, knowing that it may require the revision of his views at some stage in his experience with the data involved. At length he believes that he has sufficient evidence to draw a conclusion, from which he may proceed to other investigations based upon the conclusions already reached.

The important thing to keep in mind about the scientific method is that its validity is restricted to the realm of observable, measurable data. Science is interested in what things are, how they may be taken apart and put together in different ways, and what can be done with them. This last is, of course, the field of technology. Modern man has produced a remarkable civilization by his application of the investigative method to the making of useful gadgets for the enrichment of life on this planet.

The scientist can neither prove nor disprove the truth of the Bible. He may help us immeasurably in the effort to discover and understand important facts about it. Archaeology, for example, has greatly enriched our appreciation of the Bible by uncovering much of the civilization of the biblical world. The science of language study has provided fresh insights into the meaning of passages and has given the answer to many puzzling questions. The various sciences have served the cause of biblical scholarship in countless ways. But science does not deal with the problems of ultimate meaning, with the religious issues of purpose and value. Science may describe the process by which man has emerged from primitivism, but it cannot tell us the meaning of his life or reveal his origin or destiny. When it seeks to do so, it renounces the very scientific method which is its reason for being. The scientist may indeed have convictions about ultimate reality, and those convictions may be informed by his extensive scientific knowledge. But they are in the end theological and philosophical in nature, not scientific. When the scientist talks about ultimate meaning—either for it or against it—he has ceased being a scientist and has become a man of faith, or of no faith.

The war of science and religion is now largely a curious historical phenomenon. Most biblical scholars do not think it necessary to defend the Bible against science, for they do not see the two as in conflict. They do not suppose that the Bible is the source of all knowledge, scientific as well as religious. They realize that the Bible, the divinely inspired record of God's revelation of himself through his people and supremely through his Son, is written in the thought forms of the people of its time. The fact that the writers were inspired by God did not give them advance knowledge of those matters which in God's own time man was permitted to discover by employing the scientific method.

Perhaps an example will illuminate the point. The writer of the eighth Psalm celebrated the wonder of God, who, having made the splendor of the heavens, "the moon and the stars," still is mindful of man. The man who wrote that psalm did not know as much about astronomy as any sixth grader in the public schools today. But he knew God, and he knew to make the great affirmation, which science can neither prove nor disprove—that the Creator of this vastness is aware of and concerned about man.

This is not to say that there are no problems with respect to religion and science. It is to say that man, proceeding from the experience of faith in God through Christ on the one hand, and working with scientific data in the world of phenomena on the other hand, need feel no irreconcilable conflict. It is like a man trying to decide whether to wear his shirt or his pants. He needs them both. Indeed, if science has done nothing else for religion, it has made people who believe in God realize that the God they believe in is greater than their greatest conception of him.

The question of miracles is of special interest to people who are impressed with the law-abiding nature of the universe. This dependability of the natural order is the basis of the scientific method. Because there is a predictable cause-effect reality in the natural world, science tends to look askance at the idea of the natural law being interrupted by the intervention of miracle. However, it should be pointed out that contemporary scientists are a good deal less sure of the notion of the mechanical regularity of the natural order than their predecessors generally were. Today's scientist is apt to be something of a mystic about this because he knows enough to know that there is much in the natural world which cannot be explained by science.

The man of faith may be less troubled by miracles because he believes that the God who made the universe may, if he chooses, interrupt the law by which it operates. Further, he sees that the God who created the universe and ordained its order may intervene by means of a natural law not familiar to man. The scientist might then observe that we are only admitting that there are natural laws which we still do not understand. For example, he might argue that once man assumed that storm and drought belonged to the realm of the miracle. Now we can explain such phenomena in terms of natural law. We can follow the approach of a hurricane and accurately predict its destructive path. We even designate it by a girl's name!

But much of the discussion about miracles misses the point made in the Bible. One should not read back into the mind of the biblical writer an understanding of miracles which confines them to the realm of the supernatural imposing itself upon and interrupting the natural law. The Bible understands miracles as the wonderful demonstration of God's power on any occasion to achieve his purpose. Whether this is done through events that have a natural or a supernatural explanation is not the crucial point from the biblical perspective. It is that God has acted in a particular situation to accomplish his purpose.

For example, the Bible offers no explanation of the causes of the plagues which afflicted the Egyptians when they refused to let the children of Israel go free except the simple declaration that they were acts of God. Attempts to explain them in terms of natural phenomena are somewhat beside the point. The point is that Israel understood these happenings as evidences that God was involved in their destiny and was determined that they should leave Egypt.

Or look at the seven "signs" reported in John's Gospel. These, beginning with changing water into wine at the wedding feast in Cana and ending with the raising of Lazarus at Bethany, are offered as evidence that Jesus is the Christ. It would not have occurred to John to raise the question of natural phenomena. He cited these as extraordinary evidences that Jesus is the Christ.

This, of course, does not provide any neat or pat answers to the multitude of questions that trouble people about miracles. It does, however, make many of these questions irrelevant. If God is God then, whether he intervenes in our affairs in accordance with natural law or by superseding it, is less significant than the fact that he does.

The Bible as Literature

Even a casual examination of the writing in the Bible will reveal that it is composed of a variety of types of literature. A closer look will show that the writing is uneven in its literary value, some parts being highly exalted expressions that inspire the admiration of the most exacting literary critic. Other parts remind the reader of the pages of a census report. There is moving, eloquent prose as well as poetry, and there is also simple narrative relating the acts of a person or a people as they participate in the plan of God. There is drama as well, and many "sermons," both in the Old Testament and the New, communicate God's Word in terms that are as relevant today as they were the day they were written.

It helps us to appreciate the Bible as literature if we know some of the characteristics of the ancient Hebrews who wrote the Bible. For one thing, they were fond of picturesque, figurative, and symbolic language. Our prosaic, literalistic Western minds have a difficult time with the imagery of the Bible. Imagination was the vehicle of the Hebrew's thought. When he wished to convey a truth, he drew a word picture. We have no problem accepting this when we read that Jesus described himself as the "door," or "Good Shepherd," or "light." But at other times we seem to strain at an image in an effort to turn it into a literal fact.

Another feature of biblical literature is its lack of interest in preciseness. Above we have spoken of the influence of the scientific method upon our thinking. The Hebrew was not that much interested in factual data. He was concerned with the accuracy of the truth itself. People looking for something to "pick at" in the Bible can find inconsistencies in numbers, dates, names, and places. They sometimes think that they have struck a mortal blow against the Bible by such trivial nonsense.

Again, there is a good deal of duplication of material in the Bible. This is in part because more than one person or group reported the same period or event, and it is due in part to the fact that these people did not have our modern notions about copyright materials. They felt free to quote anyone at any time without permission or acknowledgment that they were quoting. The fact that they did so in no way lessens the validity or divine authority of what they wrote.

Christianity is a religion of the Book. We are a people of the Book.

It is an intensely human book. It is a book about historical persons, places, and events; but it is history written from a specific perspective. That perspective is that God has acted in and through the events reported and that he has overseen the reporting of those events. The words of the Bible are in this sense God's words. How we believe he watched over and directed the writing and preservation of the Bible is the subject of the next chapter.

---

[1] *Annual of the Southern Baptist Convention,* 1963, p. 270.

CHAPTER TWO

How God
Is Related to
the Bible

"The Word of God in the words of men" is often quoted as a pithy saying that expresses how God is related to the Bible. It is an over-simplification, as are most epigrams; but it does recognize some pivotal issues concerning the nature of revelation and inspiration. One is that it takes into account the human element in the Bible. The people of God, out of whose history the Bible came, bore a certain continuity with the life of mankind generally. They ate and drank, loved and hated, fought and were victorious or defeated, suffered and died like other people. They shared the limitations and prejudices of their contemporaries. The fact that they were God's people did not give them special insight in mundane affairs. It would be hard to demonstrate, for instance, that the writer of the book of Jonah knew more about geography than did the pagan residents of Nineveh.

The Bible is written in the words of men. It is not some special supernatural language, but the everyday words of everyday conversation—the Old Testament almost entirely in Hebrew, the New Testament in Greek. The styles of the writers differ according to their personal nature and the circumstances under which they wrote. Jeremiah, the lamenting prophet, wrote like himself and not like the writer of the Song of Solomon.

This human side of the Bible has long been recognized by those who read and study it. In 1963, for example, the Southern Baptist Convention adopted a statement called "Baptist Ideals," in which it said in part about the Bible: "The Holy Bible was written by men divinely inspired and is the record of God's revelation of Himself to man." [1] This statement takes a firm stand concerning the divine origin of the Scriptures, but it also recognizes that the writers were men with the freedom to be men and not mere tape recorders.

If the Bible were only another book written about God and man's relationship with him, it would have no special significance for the Christian. Obviously, there are many such fine books. What gives the Bible decisive meaning to us? It is God's word to us, and in it we meet God's revelation. In this chapter we shall examine the meaning of revelation and inspiration, and then comment on why the Bible continues to be for us the authoritative rule and guide of faith and practice.

The Meaning of Revelation

Revelation means disclosure. It is an unveiling. Applied to God, revelation means simply that God has made himself known to us. But the image of an unveiling may convey a conception of revelation contrary to the Bible's meaning. When the Bible speaks of God revealing himself, it does not mean that at some point in history he drew back the curtain and permitted man to gaze into a holy of holies where the Almighty resided in solitary splendor like an Oriental potentate. That kind of static, mechanical, "frozen" concept of revelation is entirely unbiblical.

In the Bible, revelation is action. It is action originating in God and taking place in the life of his people. Revelation is more than a sign reading: "Caution: God at work!" It *is* God working. Revelation is not a tableau on a stage which at some dramatic moment is shown by raising the curtain. It is God, the chief actor, out in the audience and each person in the audience himself a part of the action.

Perhaps an illustration or two from the Scriptures will illuminate. The Hebrew recoiled from efforts to concretize the nature of God in any kind of graven image. To assume that man could draw a picture or sculpt a statue that would capture the nature of God was the height of foolish idolatry. How, then, could one know what God is like? One saw his works. One "caught him in flight," experienced his presence by experiencing what he did. Thus, in Isaiah 52:10 we read,

"The Lord has bared his holy arm before the eyes of all the nations" (RSV), and Isaiah 53:1 asks, "To whom has the arm of the Lord been revealed?" (RSV). This vivid figure of the bared arm is precisely what the Bible means by God revealing himself. The bared arm is the symbol of action, participation, power. God is not playing "hide and seek" with us, waiting in some verdant bower for man to discover him. It is man, according to Genesis, who is hiding from God. God comes searching for him, calling his name. "Where art thou, Adam?" is the essence of revelation, for it is always God who takes the initiative. Revelation is God's self-disclosure by coming to man and participating in man's situation.

Romans 1:17 is a familiar and extremely significant statement of the meaning of revelation. Here Paul wrote: "For in it [the gospel] the righteousness of God is revealed through faith for faith" (RSV). What is the gospel? It is not merely the *announcement* that certain world-changing, redemptive things have happened. As the preceding verse (1:16) makes clear, the gospel is the "happening" itself. Paul is not ashamed of the gospel, for it is "the dynamic action of God" unto salvation for all who have faith. Through this dynamic action, which we describe by calling it "gospel," God's righteousness is revealed. What is God's "righteousness"? It is his way of expressing his nature, his God-ness. It is his way of responding to man's condition of lostness and alienation by getting involved in our life, which he did in the incarnation. In Christ, God has revealed himself completely.

Let us see, now, if we are beginning to bring the biblical meaning of revelation into focus. First, man does not "discover" God, as Columbus found the New World or Madame Curie discovered radium. We neither "stumble" upon him nor do we find him at the end of a series of experiments. God is not hiding. It is man's sin that veils his eyes. As Isaiah put it, "The Lord's hand is not shortened, that it cannot save, or his ear dull, that it cannot hear; but your iniquities have made a separation between you and your God, and your sins have hid his face from you" (59:1–2, RSV).

Second, God does not allow himself to be viewed as one would stand and gaze at a work of art. God reveals himself by what he does in, among, and through his people for their redemption. The ultimate expression of his "doing" is his incarnation in Christ. His revelation is not primarily in a series of press releases, or in decisions handed down in writing from his celestial judgment bar or thundered from the battlements of glory. His revelation is first and foremost in what he has done and in why he has done it. As one has put it, "What we find in the Bible is not an accumulation of data about God, but rather a living God in living relationship with living people." [2]

The scene of revelation is the human plane, the life of God's people. And God has been here among us not to put himself on display like a performing gymnast before the admiring eyes of spectators, but as participant in the affairs of man. And as God has been at work here—preaching, healing, rebuking, comforting, and loving—through those who did these things in his name, the revelation of God has been given.

Sometimes he revealed himself even through one who was an unknowing agent of revelation. Thus did Isaiah assess the role of a foreign power at one juncture of Israel's life when he quoted God as saying, "Ah, Assyria, the rod of my anger, the staff of my fury!" (10:5, RSV). This pagan nation was not a willing implement of the Almighty: "But he does not so intend, and his mind does not so think" (10:7, RSV). Or, again two centuries later when the Persian Cyrus in 538 B.C. issued the edict permitting the Jewish captives in Babylon to return to their homeland, the prophet addressed this unbelieving foreign despot in these words: " 'I gird you, though you do not know me' " (Isa. 45:5, RSV). But through whatever instrument the revelation came it was never a sterile, abstract pronouncement. It always came in and through a life situation.

Subsequently, the revelation was incorporated in the records written by men whom God chose and directed to express in word pictures the acts of his revelation. These records are the Bible. But neither the original revelation nor the record of it should be thought of as something frozen, static, and inactive. The revelation is not a display case in a museum, nor is it a sacred document safely stored in the archives. It is the action of God, both past and present.

"The End of Fragments"

In his opening words, the writer of the letter to the Hebrews vividly expressed this biblical concept of the "continuous action" nature of revelation and its culmination in Christ. "When in former times God spoke to our forefathers, he spoke in fragmentary and varied fashion through the prophets. But in this final age he has spoken to us in the

Son . . . who is the effulgence of God's splendour and the stamp of God's very being" (1:1-3, NEB).[3] The care with which this introduction to the letter was composed is reflected in part by the choice of a preponderance of words all beginning with the Greek letter "p" in the opening declaration. Quite obviously, the writer wished to create an alliterative effect.

But while that particular construction of the introduction was not likely a coincidence, it was incidental when compared to the import of the writer's thought. The words are not only beautiful to read, they are a panoramic view of the history of revelation. God has spoken! Hebrew thought about speaking is much more akin to action than is our conception of it. We often unconsciously set speaking and acting as opposites. So, we think people ought to "do something about it" instead of "talking." The Hebrew did not separate the two as if they were different ways of approaching a matter. To speak was to convey more than words; it was to communicate oneself, thrust oneself into the situation. So God, the writer of this letter puts it, has acted (spoken) in fragmentary and varied fashion through the prophets.

One has to raise the question, "Why in fragmentary and varied fashion?" Is God arbitrarily giving himself out little by little, line by line? If he is the same God yesterday, today, and forever, how can this verse of Scripture declare that he spoke in "varied fashion"? Does this imply that God is one way at one time and another way at another time? No, such conclusions are wholly unwarranted. The verse is simply pointing out that the revelation of God did not come like a blinding flash, because man is unable to receive it in that way. Little by little, piece by piece, in this way and that, God spoke through the prophets.

Call the roll of these great spokesmen for God. Step up, Amos, and speak to us as you did in Bethel of Israel seven hundred and fifty years before Christ. Cry out to us the indignation of a righteous God who says, " 'I hate, I despise your feasts, and I take no delight in your solemn assemblies. . . . But let justice roll down like waters, and righteousness like an everflowing stream' " (5:21-24, RSV). That is a piece of God's message, a greatly needed piece in our day as in Amos'. But that is a fragment of revelation.

Step up, Hosea, lover of a faithless wife who deserts her husband and children to traipse off after her paramours, and tell us of the love of God for faithless Israel. Let us hear again the cry of an anguished

Redeemer: "How can I give you up, O Ephraim! How can I hand you over, O Israel! . . . My heart recoils within me, my compassion grows warm and tender" (11:8, RSV). That is a part of the revelation, "For the love of God is broader than the measure of man's mind; and the heart of the Eternal is most wonderfully kind." [4] But that is also a fragment.

Step up, Isaiah, prince of prophets who "in the year that King Uzziah died . . . saw the Lord sitting upon a throne, high and lifted up; and his train filled the temple" (6:1, RSV). Tell us how, overwhelmed by the majesty and holiness of this God of the universe, you cried: " 'Woe is me! For I am lost; for I am a man of unclean lips, and I dwell in the midst of a people of unclean lips; for my eyes have seen the King, the Lord of hosts!' " (6:5, RSV). That picture of God the Wholly Other is a much needed correction of our modern human arrogance of chumminess with "the Man Upstairs." That, too, is a part of the revelation. But it is a fragment.

Or call that fourth great spokesman for God in the eighth century B.C., Micah, and ask him for his witness. What will he say? He will take the piece from Amos, the fragment from Hosea, and the part from Isaiah; and, like fitting together three pieces of a jigsaw puzzle, he will announce: "He has showed you, O man, what is good; and what does the Lord require of you but to do justice [Amos], and to love kindness [Hosea], and to walk humbly with your God [Isaiah]?" (6:8, RSV). But even this is a fragment. Through the prophets and through the law we know but the "outskirts of his ways."

However, there came a time when he who had spoken in fragmentary and varied fashion spoke to us in his Son. It was as if all the pieces were assembled and, when put together properly, there was "the glory of God in the face of Jesus Christ" (2 Cor. 4:6). Such an analogy is defective in one respect, of course, for it was not man struggling until he got the pieces put together that revealed the likeness of God in Christ. Rather, it was when Christ appeared in the midst of those who were working with the pieces that they recognized him as the embodiment of all the parts properly assembled.

The writer of Hebrews was quite explicit about the meaning of this total revelation in Christ. He is "the stamp of God's very being." It is as if soft, pliant wax had been impressed by the royal stamp to authenticate a document. When the stamp is lifted, the image that remains in the wax is the very image of the stamp itself. So is Christ to the Father.

Hopefully, as you have been reading about the meaning of revelation some questions have arisen: Has God revealed himself nowhere else than in the Bible and supremely in his Son, Jesus Christ? Since Christ is "the stamp of God's very being," did revelation end with his coming? Since God spoke in fragmentary fashion to the prophets, does this suggest an uneven level of revelation in the Bible? How did God give out these "fragments" to those who wrote? If we have the full revelation of God in Christ, why do we need the Bible at all? Particularly, of what use is the Old Testament since all that it had to say about God, and infinitely more, is given to us in Christ? In what sense is the Bible our authoritative rule and guide of faith and conduct? Whether or not they can be satisfactorily answered, such questions deserve attention.

Revelation: General or Particular

Is God's revelation of himself confined to the biblical revelation? Christians are not agreed upon the answer. Most Christians would not be willing to say that revelation is everywhere equally valid; that is, that God speaks equally in nature, history, other religions, and in the insights of great thinkers and writers as clearly as in the Bible. Some say that God speaks nowhere except in the biblical revelation (of which the ultimate embodiment is Christ himself). But the apostle Paul appears to have held that there is such a reality as "general revelation" in nature.

This is to say that the creation bears the mark of its Creator. "The heavens declare the glory of God; and the firmament sheweth his handiwork" (Psalm 19:1). Paul took this fact to be the basis of man's universal liability for his rebellion against God. Man really could not offer the defense that he did not know better even though he had not been tutored by the Law and the Prophets. Here is the way Paul argued the case: "Ever since the creation of the world his invisible nature, namely, his eternal power and deity, has been clearly perceived in the things that have been made. So they are without excuse" (Rom. 1:20, RSV).

But neither the psalmist nor Paul would ever argue that since we have nature we do not need the Bible. They knew that while nature raises questions about ultimate meaning which cannot be answered without God, nature does not provide the answers to those questions. No one can discern the character of God from studying nature. While it may give us lovely sunsets and gorgeous rainbows, it also produces tornadoes, earthquakes, tidal waves, and droughts that cause crop failures and starvation. God cannot be "explained" by nature; nature is explained by God.

Similar conclusions have to be reached about history. God may be traced through the course of world history. He has left his footprints here. But history, like nature, is a poor arena for the revelation of God because it is a mixed and confused story of human violence, greed, and lust for power. We would not deny all evidence of God outside the biblical revelation. What we Christians believe is that in this particular record of revelation, the Bible, God has spoken uniquely.

Christ, the Ultimate Revelation

If one asks, Did revelation end with the incarnation? the answer for the Christian is yes. God has nothing further to give. How can you give more when you have given all? This is what "in-carnation" means. God clothed himself in flesh. He incarnated, "enfleshed," himself. He can offer nothing greater.

But at this point a very important consideration arises. It is that our *apprehension* of the revelation in Christ is quite incomplete. Indeed, the grasp of its dimensions varies greatly in a single lifetime of Christian experience. Let us say with Paul (whose apprehension of the revelation was doubtless considerably greater than our own), "Now I know in part" (1 Cor. 13:12).

Jesus himself recognized that his disciples' understanding of the revelation was partial. In the sense that he did what he was sent to do, to give his life as an expiation of our sin, he finished his work. But in another sense he could not finish it. Nor is it finished yet. Sitting in the upper room on that fateful night with the climax of the Father's eternal purpose rushing upon him, he talked to his disciples about the future and their continuing need for understanding the revelation. " 'I have yet many things to say to you, but you cannot bear them now. When the Spirit of truth comes, he will guide you into all the truth' " (John 16:12–13, RSV). Is he not still guiding us? The revelation is complete. God has not changed his mind about anything. He has no need to do so. But our understanding of what he is saying—indeed, what he does say to each generation—is unfolding and growing. This is the reason why certain great issues, such as equality of opportunity and brotherhood among peoples, come to be burning concerns of Christian conscience in a particular era. Our apprehension of the revelation grows. It is all part of our grasping the reality which has already come and is among us.

Revelation Is Uneven

If God spoke in "fragmentary and varied fashion" through the prophets, then we ought not to be troubled by the realization that all of the fragments are not of equal merit when placed beside the ultimate revelation, Jesus Christ. As the statement from the 1963 meeting of the Southern Baptist Convention puts it: "The criterion by which the Bible is to be interpreted is Jesus Christ." [5] Now, if we interpret certain passages by the criterion of Jesus Christ, we have to conclude that the level of disclosure of God in those instances is very low. There are psalms, for example, in which the author prayed against his enemies and asked God never to forgive them. There are other passages where the writer rejoiced to think of enemy babies having their heads bashed against a rock. Put that alongside the Sermon on the Mount! It is quite a relief to realize that one can love and revere the Bible and believe that it is the inspired record of God's revelation without having to defend those passages which violate the Spirit of Christ.

Is it not better to end the moral confusion by honestly recognizing that the understanding of what God was communicating through revelation is not everywhere of equal value in the Bible? This is not a simple matter of saying that the Old Testament represents the pre-Christian revelation while the New Testament gives the Christian understanding of God and his relationship to man. Obviously this is not a sufficient explanation, for there are passages like Isaiah 6; 9; 53 and Psalms 1; 23; 42; 51; 90; 103, to list only a few of the magnificent mountain peaks of Old Testament revelation.

If someone is tempted to say, "Ah ha, you want to pick and choose and make up your own Bible," we must protest: No, the Bible is the record of God's self-disclosure in the historical events (some crude and terrible) of his people and in their thought-life (some of it far beneath the standard of Christian ethics or theology). But whether or not that record of revelation is consistent with the fulness of God's self-disclosure can be determined only by laying it alongside the revelation of Jesus Christ.

If one says, "Well, of course the Hebrews were children of their own age and life was often hard and brutal, but they had higher moral and theological concepts than their neighbors," we would answer: To be sure. This is precisely the point. Compare the Hebrew concept of God with that of the Canaanites, and you realize how very advanced was the Hebrew's religious understanding. But does that not confirm what our minds and hearts tell us is true, namely, that there was a growing apprehension of God's self-disclosure? If we believe that in Jesus Christ "all the fulness of God was pleased to dwell" (Col. 1:19, RSV), then we are prepared to test all revelation by him.

How Did God Inspire the Bible?

If God "gave himself out in fragmentary fashion," piece by piece, and guided those through whom and for whom he acted to set the record of it down, how did it take place? This is a question about inspiration of the Scriptures. To begin with, it may be helpful to distinguish between revelation and inspiration. We have seen that revelation is God's self-disclosure achieved in and through and for man. Revelation has taken place in historical events, particularly in the history of the people of the covenant, and supremely in Jesus Christ. Of this revelation the Bible is the record. That record came about because God inspired—"breathed into," "in-spirited"—those who wrote. Revelation is the truth of God emerging out of his relationship with man; inspiration is the impulse to preserve it and hand it on. The two were interdependent. "For without revelation there would be no point in inspiration. Without inspiration, on the other hand, revelation would die with the first person to whom it came." [6]

But what about this "divine impulse to record the revelation"? In what sense is it unique? Are men not "inspired" to write or paint or sculpt or sing or play? Yes, but the uniqueness of biblical inspiration lies in the nature of the message communicated. It was the message of God's self-disclosure. It was the story of God's redemption of man.

Such a message called for conveyers specially prepared and supervised. The assignment of recording this message was put in the hands of men who were moved and directed by God's Spirit.

We do not believe that they were mere automatic transcribers of divine dictation. Their language, style, and thought reflect the individual differences that would be expected to exist between people separated by centuries of time and wide variations in cultural and spiritual development. Belief in the inspiration of the Scriptures does not require that originally there had to be a letter-perfect Bible. Inspiration does not mean dictation. It means that in the Bible we have a reliable record of God's revelation because God himself inspired "holy men of old" to put it down, although we see no evidence that he violated their freedom as persons when he moved them to do so.

From this point of view, then, many controversies over inspiration are futile and pointless exercises. The fact that Ehud, a judge of Israel, was left-handed, or that the Mahlites and the Mushites were descendants of Merari seem hardly weighty enough matters to argue about whether or not the words were inspired. They are simple reports of facts which are not the main point of the revelation of God. Nor do we need to engage in mental gymnastics to try to reconcile certain apparent confusions of place names, dates, and numbers in various accounts of the same events. The confusion may be in textual errors made in copying that was done before the time of printing, or it may lie in our failure to understand all that is written. But if, as we believe, inspiration is the "divine impulse to record the revelation" in human language and thought, then we need not be tied to some mechanical, tape-recorder concept of inspiration. We can and do have confidence in the Bible as truth without feeling that we are unfaithful to the Scriptures if we do not place "Behold, his bedstead was a bedstead of iron" (Deut. 3:11) and "God is love" on the same level.

Rule and Guide of Faith and Conduct

In what sense is the Bible, as Baptists are fond of describing it, our "rule and guide of faith and conduct"? If we have the complete revelation of God in Jesus Christ, why do we need the Bible at all? Particularly, why cling to the Old Testament?

Suppose we take the latter question first. It is interesting that the first great heresy to threaten the life of the church involved this very issue. About A.D. 140 a man named Marcion, an influential figure in the church at Rome, sought to eliminate all Hebrew influence from the Christian religion. He wished to turn Christianity into gnosticism, which denied, among other things, the humanity of Christ. In order to eradicate Hebrew influence in Christianity, Marcion sought to have the Old Testament taken out of the Bible. He believed it to be a hindrance to the true faith. Needless to say, the church got rid of Marcion and kept the Old Testament!

The Old Testament was retained for the very good reason that it is part of the continuous record of revelation. God did not just begin with man at the time of the coming of Christ. He had been dealing with him, specifically and particularly, through the life of the covenant people. The record of that relationship is a part of the indispensable heritage of our faith.

But is the Bible more than a record of something that happened long ago? Since Christ has come and we know about him, why do we need the Bible? Indeed, it appears that none of the Gospels were written until several decades after his resurrection. Why did they write them at all? Why not just depend upon the faithful believers passing the message on by word of mouth from one generation to another? In what sense do we need the Bible to be such a rule and guide?

We need the biblical record as a constant guide to which we can refer and by which we can correct our errors. Is not Christ that invariable "North Star"? Of course he is, but our relationship to Christ is itself imperfect and incomplete. How shall we evaluate our understanding of him—through the accumulated experience of the church, through our personal experience with him, or by the record of him in the Bible? Well, all of these—the witness of the community of faith (church), the witness of the inner personal experience, and the Bible—are relevant. But we retain the Bible as a corrective both of the church and of our personal understanding of our experience with Christ.

If we discard the Bible, we are thrown back upon the understanding of the revelation which each generation has in turn. God's work in Christ is too tremendous for any generation to grasp its total meaning. Any age succeeds in passing on only that which it has itself been able to appropriate and make vital. Anders Nygren has illuminated this point: "If each generation had nothing more to draw on than the tradition which its predecessor had passed on, progressive impoverishment would be inevitable. The result would be the continual dilution of the message." [7]

But with the Bible, every succeeding generation stands fresh before the record, having access to the message in its original form. God can speak to us immediately through the record of his revelation of himself. While the Christian is bound in his faith by the message of the Bible, he can be unbound by the traditions and interpretations of men. That is one reason why the Bible remains as our rule and guide of faith and practice.

Furthermore, we claim the Bible for our guide in matters of faith because it is more than a record of something that has happened. It is also, by being such a message, a means of the continuation of the very transforming work which it reports. Consider this illustration given by Dr. Nygren:

When in World War II the news came one day that Denmark and Norway were free of Nazi occupation, it was a great day for all of Scandinavia. "Denmark is free! Norway is free!" It was more than a mere piece of news. It was a stirring message about liberation. Now, more than thirty years later, we may read the record of that liberation and view it only as a fact of history. But when it happened, it was more than a mere fact. While it had an objective reality, it had also a subjective reality. It stirred the heart of every true Scandinavian. It caused his heart to swell with pride and patriotism. It literally changed his own personal situation, even though he might have been unconnected with the oppression of the occupation. [8]

The Bible is both an announcement of something that happened and also a stirring witness to each one who gets involved in the message. The liberation did not happen just "once upon a time," but it continues to happen wherever the message is faithfully preached and heard in repentance and faith. There is something about the news which the Bible reports that causes men to say, "This is for me. The liberation of which this book speaks is my own liberation in Christ." For this reason, the Bible is as relevant today as when it was first recorded under the guidance of the Spirit of God. It tells of man's universal need and of God's universal redemptive love.

In this chapter we have tried to wend our way carefully, honestly, and reverently through the sometimes controversial and highly-charged field of revelation, inspiration, and authority. With the prayer that what has been said may be helpful, we turn next to what hopefully will be more factual in nature. But do not let that cause you to skip the next chapter. It ought not to be dull. Geography and history are really fascinating true stories about places and people.

[1] *Annual of the Southern Baptist Convention,* 1963, p. 270.

[2] Robert McAfee Brown, *The Bible Speaks to You* (Philadelphia: Westminster Press, 1966), p. 41.

[3] © The Delegates of the Oxford University Press and the Syndics of the Cambridge University Press, 1961.

[4] Frederick W. Faber and Lizzie S. Tourjee, "There's a Wideness in God's Mercy," *Baptist Hymnal,* p. 48.

[5] *Annual of S. B. C., op. cit.,* p. 270.

[6] *The Layman's Bible Commentary* (Richmond: John Knox Press, 1959), I, 21.

[7] Anders Nygren, *The Significance of the Bible for the Church* (Philadelphia: Fortress Press, 1963), p. 10.

[8] Nygren, *op. cit.,* pp. 4–5.

CHAPTER THREE

Places and People
of the
Old Testament
Part I—From the Patriarchs
to Sinai (2000-1280 B.C.)

The Bible should be viewed from the perspective of what God was doing in and through the history of a particular people occupying a specific arena. That is the approach of the Bible itself. It is not simply reporting what happened, but explaining the meaning of events in the light of God's redemptive purpose. The principal "character" is God himself and our primary focus is on him. The first two chapters of this book sought to illuminate this thesis, and we shall come back to it again and again, particularly in the study of the Bible's major theme.

Understanding and appreciation grow, however, in the study of the setting where the action took place and the people who were involved, both Israel and those among whom they lived. We do not turn to geography and history of the Bible simply out of intellectual curiosity, but because the meaning of the message from God is in part known through the places and people concerned.

Where It Happened

Geography has been called "the field on which the game of history is played." [1] All of biblical history took place in a relatively small but crucially important area no more than five hundred miles from north to south and one thousand miles east to west. This was the cradle of the civilizations of our heritage. Look at the shaded areas on the map appearing on the opposite page. Note that they form a crescent, one tip being the Nile Valley in Egypt and the other the Tigris-Euphrates Valley in Mesopotamia. Joining the two, rising in an elliptical arch, are Palestine, Syria, and the areas of the upper Tigris and Euphrates. Historians have called this the Fertile Crescent for the obvious reason that climate, rainfall, and soil combined to make it productive enough to support settled populations where civilization could develop.

Under the curve of the crescent, forming its inner perimeter, lay vast desert wastes stretching down across the Arabian Peninsula. Here life was perennially meager and hard, for the arid climate made an agrarian culture impossible. Instead, the people who wandered over the area grazing their flocks and herds lived a nomadic existence, finding pasture during the winter months but having to remain close by the desert oases in the dry summer. These nomads were Semitic in race, the forebears of Israel. From time to time they invaded the Fertile Crescent, overthrowing existing cultures and subsequently settling down to establish their own, which were often overturned by successive waves of invasions from north or south.

Above the curve of the crescent, along its northern and eastern boundaries, a series of rugged mountain ranges and plateaus forms a semicircle. From this perimeter of civilization, periodic invasions also came. For example, a coalition of people from the Zagros Mountains swept down into the Tigris-Euphrates Valley and overthrew the government near the end of the third millennium B.C., only to be overturned themselves by a resurgence of an earlier culture. Later the Hurrians (Old Testament Horites) came down from the mountains northeast of the Fertile Crescent and established themselves in central Mesopotamia, attaining great power in the kingdom of Mitanni during the fifteenth and fourteenth centuries.

To the northwest lay the region which was later to be known as Asia Minor, the home of Indo-European peoples who were likewise to affect the fortunes of the people of the Old Testament. In this area the mighty Hittite Empire rose to such power in the second millennium B.C. that it stood as the chief rival to Egypt at a time of Egyptian greatness.

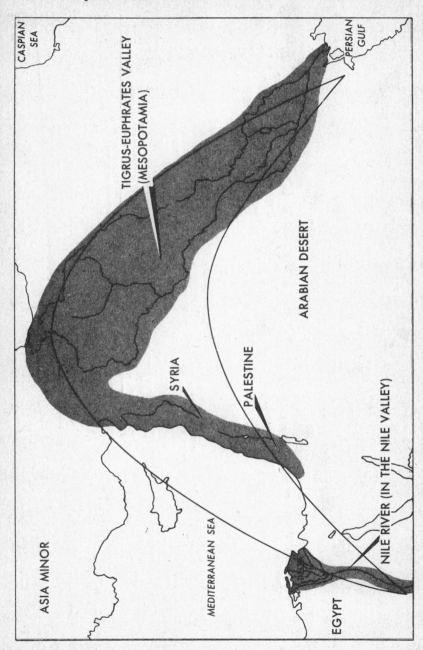

The Nile—Lifeline of Egypt

At the southwestern end of the crescent lay Egypt, the other great power of ancient civilization. Unlike Mesopotamia, whose borders lay exposed, Egypt was protected by natural barriers from outside influences and invasion. To her north was the Mediterranean Sea, to the south the cataracts of the Nile River, and vast stretches of desert lay on either side. For centuries the country was sealed off and comparatively unexposed to the upheavals caused by invasion of new peoples. As a consequence, except for a few occasions when inner weakness and turmoil made it possible for Asiatics to gain control, the civilization of Egypt remained relatively stable for more than two thousand years.

The Nile River is literally the life of Egypt. For seven hundred and fifty miles running north to the Mediterranean, the Nile River provides the only source of water to sustain life. For the most of that distance, the river flows through a narrow trough of limestone cliffs. This was known as Upper Egypt. Near the location of the modern city of Cairo (ancient Memphis), the Nile spreads out into a delta, forming a fertile triangle crossed by many streams which bear the Nile's waters to the sea. The delta constituted Lower Egypt. At one time the areas were separated into two kingdoms, though they were almost always one.

The annual overflow of the Nile brought life-giving moisture and fertility. Rainfall was sparse, varying from eight inches annually near the mouth of the Nile to practically none at all in Upper Egypt. It is little wonder that the ancient Egyptian regarded the Nile as a god. Every year, from July to October, the Nile rises, fed by its tributaries in the heart of Africa. Early in November the waters begin to recede, and in ancient times as soon as possible thereafter the seed would be planted in the moist alluvial soil. If the annual flood was adequate, the country might expect an abundant harvest sufficient to make her the world's granary. But so delicate was the balance between plenty and famine that a failure of the Nile could mean complete disaster. One can thus understand the significance of the achievement of Joseph whose careful planning as prime minister saved Egypt from starvation during seven years of want.

Early a system of irrigation was developed to extend the time of the soil's fertility, but always it is the Nile which is the source of life. The visitor to Egypt is startled by the contrast between green fields where the Nile waters the soil and the barren sand where there is no irrigation. There is no gradual change from green growth to brown barrenness. Where the water stops, the green fields end. It is like a lawn surrounded by brown pavement.

Palestine-Syria

Take one more glance at the outline map. Between the Egyptian end of the Fertile Crescent and the broad arch at the top which comprises the wide upper Mesopotamian Valley lies a narrow strip never more than a hundred miles, and generally only about forty miles, wide. This is Palestine-Syria, the area in which Israel lived as a nation literally at the crossroads of the ancient world. Geographically, Palestine was the connection, a land bridge, between the two great cradles of civilization. All major land and sea routes converged upon this tiny narrow strip. The armies of the great empires crossed and recrossed this soil. Only when Egypt and the Mesopotamian powers were weak or preoccupied with internal problems could the peoples of Palestine hope to attain major eminence as political states. The development of Israel as the people of the covenant took place in this situation of being between the two great centers of world power.

The northern part of this land bridge between Egypt and Asia was known as Syria, an area dominated by Phoenicians and Aramaeans. The Phoenicians occupied the coastland of Syria and became famous seafaring people. Although they were never a part of Israel, important trade agreements existed between the two nations, as in the days of King Solomon and King Hiram of Tyre. The inland part of Syria was inhabited by the Aramaean kingdom of Damascus. It figures prominently in the history of Israel, primarily as an arch foe.

The lower coastline of Palestine was occupied by another group of Israel's early enemies, the Philistines. These were sea people, probably originally from Thrace and the Greek islands, including Crete. They were wily, fierce fighters who invaded Egypt about the beginning of the twelfth century B.C., and were driven out, some of them settling on the coastal plain and giving it the name Philistia. Later the name in its Greek form, "Palestine," came to be applied to the entire geographical region. The Philistines, formidable foes with weapons of iron, were almost continually enemies of Israel from the period of the Judges until the time of David. Palestine is also known in the Old Testament as Canaan, meaning "land of the purple." The name likely came from the fact that the Phoenicians were well-known in the ancient world for the manufacture of a purple dye which they made from a certain shellfish found along the coast.

At this point, let us turn our attention to the geography of Palestine itself, a tiny area averaging forty miles wide and one hundred and fifty miles "from Dan to Beersheba," north to south. It is difficult to imagine a piece of ground so small being the scene of such world-changing events. If we had been planning things, we would certainly have chosen a different locale. Why the rocky hillsides of Palestine rather than the palaces of Egypt or Babylon? As one has put it, "On the stage of world history it was the doormat on which the great empires scuffed their boots—hardly a fit place to expect to find God at work!" [2] Yet that God did choose this place and people is the startling claim of the Bible.

The Four Geographical Areas of Palestine

Look now at the outline map of Palestine appearing on the opposite page. Note that the country is divided into four geographical areas. Beginning at the Mediterranean, there is first a coastal plain with three main sections: the Plain of Acre, the Plain of Sharon, and the Plain of Philistia. The only one of these three plains over which Israel had any effective control was the Plain of Sharon which was largely wild wasteland and marsh.

The central hill region is the second area and the chief center of Israel's population and life. Composed of an almost continuous range of rugged hills rising to six thousand feet in the north, this region forms the "backbone" of western Palestine. The range rises in the Lebanon Mountains in Syria and continues down through the country into the Negeb and on into the desert. It is broken only by the Valley of Jezreel separating the hills of Galilee from those of Samaria. The Valley of Jezreel (later known by the Greek name, Esdraelon) provided a pass from the Mediterranean to the Jordan Valley. It was of strategic military importance, for through this pass marched the armies of the ancient world.

Below the Valley of Jezreel lay the hills of Samaria, interspersed with plains and meadows, a fertile area, inviting to the Israelite looking for a place to settle. There at ancient Shechem the patriarchs came and grazed their flocks and established their families. Two conspicuous mountain peaks of Samaria were Ebal and Gerizim,

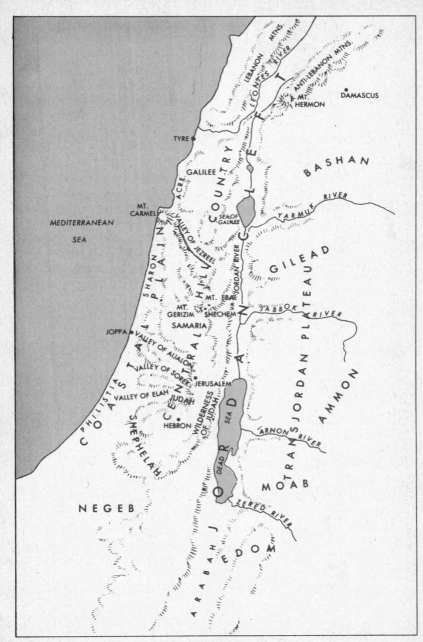

MEDITERRANEAN

SEA

LEBANON MTNS.

LEONTES RIVER

ANTI-LEBANON MTNS.

MT. HERMON

DAMASCUS

TYRE

GALILEE

ACRE

MT. CARMEL

VALLEY OF JEZREEL

SHARON

SEA OF GALILEE

BASHAN

YARMUK RIVER

GILEAD

JORDAN RIVER

CENTRAL HILL COUNTRY

MT. EBAL

MT. GERIZIM   SHECHEM

SAMARIA

JOPPA

VALLEY OF AIJALON

VALLEY OF SOREK

PLAIN

JABBOK RIVER

TRANSJORDAN PLATEAU

AMMON

VALLEY OF ELAH   JUDAH

PHILISTIA

COASTAL

JERUSALEM

SHEPHELAH

HEBRON

WILDERNESS OF JUDAH

DEAD SEA

J O R D A N

ARNON RIVER

MOAB

NEGEB

DEAD SEA

ZERED RIVER

A R A B A H

E D O M

militarily important because the main highway running through the country passed nearby. They were also important religious centers to ancient Israel because there the people gathered to ratify the covenant with God.

South of Samaria lay Judah, its hills forming a high plateau surrounded on the west by rolling foothills, called by the Israelites the Shephelah or "lowlands," dropping off to the plain. On the east lay the harsh and rocky "Wilderness of Judah." Less than half of Judah was tillable. No rivers coursed the area and water was always scarce. It was not a place inviting ease, but suggesting a life of struggle and hard work. The terrain between the hills of Judah and the Jordan River is some of the most rugged and barren in the world.

The topographical extremes of the region are nowhere more graphically demonstrated than in the third section of Palestine, the Jordan Valley. This is part of a giant cleft in the earth which begins below Mount Hermon in the north and runs through Palestine, then south through the desert, and on down to the Red Sea and into Africa. Mount Hermon, whose snows feed the Lake of Galilee, rises nine thousand feet above sea level, but so precipitous is the descent that by the time its water reaches the Lake of Galilee it has plunged to six hundred and eighty-five feet below sea level. And when the Jordan empties into the Dead Sea, it is at the deepest surface point on earth—twelve hundred and ninety feet below sea level. On either side of the Jordan River, winding like a green serpent down through the barren countryside, is the thick, lush growth known as "the Jungle of the Jordan." Jordan's waters empty into the Dead Sea which has no outlet and is consequently about 25 percent salt content.

East of the Jordan the terrain rises sharply again in the region known as the Transjordan Plateau. The northern section of this plateau was called Bashan, a fertile plain that produced an abundance of grain. South of it was the land of Gilead, from which came a famous medicinal salve, "the balm of Gilead," made from the sap of trees and exported to the ancient world. South of Gilead lay the lands of Ammon, Moab, and Edom, some of Israel's bitterest traditional enemies.

From this brief survey, the picture one gets of Canaan is that of an area of rugged, extreme contrasts. In it the Israelites matured as a people and experienced most of the events reported in the Old Testament. The country afforded few of them a life of abundance and luxury. Although the spies from the wilderness wanderings returned to the camp and reported that Canaan was a land of plenty, it must never be forgotten that that report was given by men who were used to nomadic life in a desert.

The Patriarchal Age

We have looked over the place where the events of the Old Testament happened. Now we shall scan the broad eras in which they occurred, attempting to set the Old Testament figures and events in the context of world history. At the end of the Early Bronze Age, about 2000 B.C., Mesopotamia was undergoing one of those tumultuous periods which frequently turn out to be the most creative. A thousand years of recorded history had already passed. Great empires had risen, flourished, and disappeared. Repeated onslaughts from nomadic hordes surrounding the Tigris-Euphrates Valley had overturned existing states.

The most important of these invasions was by a people called Amorites, "westerners," who for around two hundred years from 2000 B.C. overran much of the Fertile Crescent. These Semitic people from Arabia pushed out from the desert, pressing into Mesopotamia, Syria, and Palestine, toppling kingdoms as they went and eventually settling down to cease from their nomadism. One of the centers of Amorite settlement was in the vicinity of Haran, the place to which the family of Abraham moved. The times and characteristics of the Amorites are almost identical to those of the patriarchs, making it seem likely that the migration of Israel's earliest ancestors was a part of this great Amorite movement.

The Age of the Patriarchs of Israel comprises the first half of the second millennium B.C. (2000–1500). Abraham migrated from Haran to Canaan, where he wandered back and forth through the central highlands and down into the Negeb and Egypt, stopping at Shechem, Bethel, Hebron, and Beersheba, all of which were settled towns when he got there. His continued wandering throughout his life suggests the nomadic nature of his occupation. Two generations of Abraham's descendants were born and lived in Palestine. At length in a time of famine, the family moved down to Egypt where they were welcomed as settlers. Again, secular history of Semitic migrations into Canaan and often down into Egypt seeking food parallels the biblical account of Abraham, Isaac, Jacob, and Joseph.

The biblical writers, however, did not understand the migrations of the patriarchs of Israel to be merely isolated examples of a widespread population movement. The journey of Abraham was not in search of greener pastures, an easier life, or adventure. He went out in response to the command of God, who had chosen him and set him apart to be the father of the people of the covenant. He went conscious of himself as a man of destiny. He went out in faith, "not knowing whither he went."

The experiences of the patriarchs reported in Genesis are consistent with what is known of the history of this era, but the Bible sees the events through the eye of faith. God would fulfil his promises to Abraham if this man would trust him, even to making miraculous provision for the birth of an heir. Isaac would find a wife back in Haran rather than marry a woman of Canaan and possibly corrupt the stream of God's purpose. Jacob, crafty schemer, was God's choice to carry the promise rather than Esau, the worldly. The entire thrust of the biblical narrative concerning the patriarchs is that they represent God's purpose to prepare a people whom he had chosen to be the means of blessing all the families of the earth. Thus Joseph in Egypt, having been taken there as an immature boy, sold by his own brothers into slavery, and having risen to be prime minister, could say to them after many years: "It was not you who sent me here, but God" (Gen. 45:8, RSV).

Once more, secular history confirms the biblical record. In 1710 B.C., during a period of political instability, the country was invaded and conquered by a Semitic people whom the Egyptians called Hyksos, "rulers of foreign lands." The Hyksos dominated Egypt for a century and a half, during which time they built a great empire extending to Canaan and Syria. Joseph's experiences in Egypt and the subsequent settlement of the family of Jacob there are undoubtedly related to the Hyksos era. When the Hyksos were expelled by a native Egyptian regime in 1570, the Israelites no longer enjoyed a protected position and eventually were made serfs by a pharaoh "who knew not Joseph." Forced to work on royal building projects, the Israelites were being prepared for the greatest single demonstration of their entire history of God's purpose for his chosen people.

The Exodus and Wilderness Wandering

To Israel the Exodus formed the crux of history, that is, a decisive event which gave meaning to all else. Israel looked upon God's deliverance of his people from Egypt much as Christians look upon the coming of Christ. It was the crucial event which could be understood only in the conviction that God had acted. The Exodus was not the work of Moses, but of God with Moses as his instrument. His entire early life showed plainly that he was a chosen vessel: his heritage as an Israelite, his rearing in the king's court, his discipline in the wilderness whence he had fled after killing an Egyptian overseer seen beating an Israelite slave.

Yet, although the biblical account is primarily concerned to focus attention on the work of God and not upon historical detail, the Exodus is firmly established as historical. Egyptian records make no mention of the Israelite story. This is not at all surprising in view of the defeat suffered by the pharaoh at the hands of this motley band. There is good reason to believe, however, that the pharaoh of the enslavement of the Israelites was Seti I (1308–1290), and that the pharaoh of the Exodus was his successor, Rameses II (1290–1224). It was during their reigns that the cities of Raamses and Pithom, referred to in Exodus 1:11 as having been built with Israelite slave labor, were constructed. In addition, archaeological evidence indicates that the conquest of Canaan by the Israelites took place late in the thirteenth century. An Egyptian inscription from the reign of Merneptah (1224–1216), Rameses II's successor, describes an Egyptian military campaign into Palestine and reports that one of the peoples encountered were the Israelites. It is evident, then, that the Israelites were established in Canaan by 1220 B.C. Inasmuch as a generation transpired between the Exodus and the conquest, it may be concluded that the date of the Exodus is probably about 1280 B.C. (Some scholars place the Exodus at 1300 B.C. and settlement at 1200 B.C.)

Moses' training in the desert among the Kenites, a Semitic people, had prepared him to lead Israel to Sinai. Leaving Egypt, the former slaves, who now were called by God to become a nation of Chosen People, went into the Sinai Peninsula for a period of preparation. Sometime later they came to Mount Sinai, since the sixth century A.D. identified by tradition with a mountain called Jebel Musa in a range on the southern tip of the Sinai Peninsula. Here the people received the covenant embodied in the law. It was a historic and pivotal event for Israel, rivaling in importance the Exodus itself. The law was given as a means of living up to the covenant; it was to guide covenant response on the part of Israel.

---

[1] H. J. Flanders, Jr., R. W. Crapps, and D. A. Smith, *People of the Covenant* (New York: Ronald Press, 1963), p. 28.

[2] Brown, *op. cit.,* p. 41.

CHAPTER FOUR

Places and People of the Old Testament

Part II—From Tribalism to Hellenism (1280-323 B.C.)

For forty years the children of Israel dwelt in the wilderness, wandering like nomads as countless others had done before them. The Bible sees this period as a punishment for Israel's failure to follow God's bidding to enter Canaan after the twelve spies were sent into the land from Kadesh early in the Exodus period. The period also served the practical purpose of providing an opportunity for the people to develop into some semblance of unity.

Conquest and Confederation

After the death of Moses, Joshua, one of the two spies who had advised entering Canaan from the south, was made leader of Israel and the long-awaited invasion of Canaan began. The first city to fall to the invaders was Jericho, the ancient Canaanite fortress. It is often presumed that the conquest was one continuous military campaign, but this is not true. The book of Joshua reports a long, brutal, and complicated story of Israel's subjugation of Canaan. First came a campaign against the people living east of the Jordan. Three major campaigns in western Canaan are described: There was a thrust into the central highlands, followed by the overpowering of the strong

Amorite cities in the south, and subsequently a sweep into the north against a confederation of kings of northern city-states.

Some of the Israelites remained in the Transjordan region. It is likely that prior to the invasion under Joshua numerous tribal kinsmen of the Israelites were already in Canaan. These had not gone down to Egypt or, if they did go, had left when the Hyksos were expelled. Moreover, Canaanite civilization was not eradicated when the Israelites occupied the land. Much of it was not conquered, but was simply bypassed; and Canaanite strongholds remained to plague Israel for many generations. These Canaanite cities were wealthy and well fortified in comparison to the crude settlements built up by the conquering Israelites. The most accurate date for the conquest is probably around 1250–1220 B.C. (though some scholars set the conquest date as late as 1200 B.C.).

The next two centuries are known in the Bible as the period of the Judges. The tribes of Israel had settled down in Canaan, living among those already there, and establishing between themselves a kind of loose confederation. A national religious capital was established at Shiloh, where the people gathered periodically to renew their covenant vows.

During these two centuries of the era of the Judges, Israel was relatively free of interference from both Egypt and Mesopotamia, and so was able to enjoy a large measure of local autonomy. However, threats from some of Israel's neighbors periodically arose. To the east lay the kingdoms of Moab and Ammon. They had been bypassed by the invaders and presented a perennial problem to the loosely-bound confederation of individual tribes. About the middle of this period of confederation, a major threat was posed by the arrival of the Philistines. These seafaring peoples invaded the southern part of Canaan and established themselves along the seacoast in a confederacy of five cities (Gaza, Ashkelon, Ashdod, Ekron, and Gath). Employing weapons of iron superior to the bronze weapons of the Israelites, the Philistines were threatening to destroy Israel as the period of the Judges closed in 1020 B.C.

In the book of Judges, which relates the history of these two centuries, the names of twelve judges are reported. Some of the better known are Deborah, Barak, Gideon, Jephthah, and Samson. The judges were not elected leaders, but rather arose from time to time as charismatic figures gifted with some unusual quality that caused their fellow Hebrews to recognize and rally around them as leaders. They might have been local or regional figures, not accepted by all the tribes. The title "judge" is something of a misnomer, for their role was not primarily judicial but was more apt to be military. They gave the little nation leadership against its enemies. Perhaps the story of one of the judges, Samson, is the Bible's most vivid illustration of great God-given powers being perverted and wasted in unbridled self-indulgence. Samson came near the end of the period when Israel was seriously threatened by the Philistines.

The United Kingdom (1020–922 B.C.)

The Philistine problem was far more serious than the periodic border raids between the tribes of Israel and their neighbors. With their iron weapons, these invaders from the sea arrived on the southern coast of Canaan. Having been repulsed from Egypt early in the twelfth century B.C., they continued to make encroachments into the land of Israel. The career of Samuel marked the end of the era of the Judges and the beginning of the monarchy. This remarkable man was a combination of judge, prophet, and priest and represents the best of all three.

At this same time, Israel also began to be threatened by a development in the northeast. A new wave of invasions from Arabia brought the Aramaeans, an aggressive, warring people, to Israel's border in the north. There they established a powerful nation with its center at Damascus. This nation, Aram or Syria, became one of Israel's arch foes.

A strong central government was needed for survival. Samuel had mixed feelings about anointing Saul king. On the one hand, he saw the demand for a king as evidence of Israel's apostasy. On the other, he saw the tall handsome young Benjamite son of Kish as God's chosen instrument. So he anointed him the first king of Israel. The old order was passing. The little nation's system of local autonomy, each tribe coming to the others' defense when stirred up by some heroic figure, was now outmoded by the threat of Philistine and Syrian power. In 1020 B.C., Israel took a king.

Living at Gibeah in a court singularly unpretentious, Saul began his reign in humility and with great promise. The later pomp and splendor of David and Solomon were unknown to Saul. He had no harem, levied no regular taxes, conscripted no troops. At first Saul enjoyed great success against the Philistines and other of Israel's enemies. But he declined tragically, both spiritually and emotionally, and finally fell on his own sword after a defeat in battle.

The aging Samuel had long since become disenchanted with Saul. He may never have been altogether in favor of him, but Saul's mental decline must have been alarming to the nation's leaders. Samuel now anointed Saul's successor, as God led him to do. The next king was not to be a son of Saul but a youth named David, son of Jesse, a Bethlehemite. As God had directed Samuel to Saul, now he gave him divine guidance to search until he found the one whom God had chosen to succeed Saul.

A period of overlapping between the latter days of Saul and the beginning of David's reign was marked by David's rising popularity, his continued loyalty to Saul, and Saul's bitter jealousy of the young man he had come to fear and hate. Fleeing from Saul's insane attempts upon his life, David became a kind of Robin Hood, a popular hero living in mountain hideouts and gathering followers from among those disenchanted with Saul's leadership. In 1000 B.C., after a crushing defeat at the hands of the Philistines, King Saul took his own life, and David became king.

During the next forty years under his phenomenal leadership, Israel enjoyed her golden age. No strong empire was on the international scene. Egypt was no longer a threat. The Hittite Empire had been destroyed in the northwest. Assyria had not yet come to full strength in the northeast. Saul had borne the brunt of the transition from a confederation of tribes to the monarchy. The time was ripe, and David was the appropriate instrument.

David's career is divided into three periods. For the first two years after Saul's death, he reigned in Hebron over Judah only. Then he was crowned king of all Israel. Later, he moved the capital to Jerusalem, where for thirty-three years he used his enormous abilities to give Israel her finest hour.

The dimensions of this man's personality continue to engage our attention after three thousand years. The Bible makes no effort to conceal his character. Brilliant strategist, fearless fighter, ruthless foe, tender and irresistible lover, gifted administrator, hard as nails but mystical and devout, loyal to his friends, unable to cope with his family, sinner and saint locked together in the same manly figure—all of this and infinitely more was David. But the Bible sees him primarily as the bearer of the covenant. As the covenant had been identified with Abraham and circumcision, and with Moses and Sinai, so also was it identified with King David. The house of David became the symbol of God's promise to Israel. The line of David would last forever. From the loins of David would come God's Deliverer. Here is clearly a pivotal figure in the Bible.

David's death in 961 B.C. was followed by court intrigue from which Solomon, son of David by Bathsheba, emerged as successor. What David had established on the strength of his personal magnetism Solomon enlarged by careful alliance with foreign powers and favorable trade agreements. A modernized army, numerous fortifications (such as at Megiddo), the building of a merchant fleet manned by Phoenician sailors, the construction of a refinery for smelting copper, and the importing and exporting of goods brought wealth and power which made the expression "Solomon in all his glory" more than a byword. He became fabulously rich. Literature, particularly wisdom writings, flourished, along with other cultural works. But his most lasting achievement from the biblical perspective was the building of the Temple in Jerusalem, combining Phoenician architecture with the simple austerity of Hebrew concepts of worship. Seven years were taken to complete the construction of the Temple, and Solomon may have done even better for himself because he also had a palace built which required thirteen years to complete.

Two Struggling Nations (922–722 B.C.)

The splendor of Solomon was not without its price, however. His harem of foreign women, whom he married to seal political alliances, was offensive to many. These women brought their own religions with them, and Solomon permitted the worship of these foreign deities. His heavy burdens of taxation and forced labor, requiring one month in three to be given in the king's service, caused deep resentment in the fiercely independent Hebrews. The common man began to feel that the magnificence of the court was largely at his expense. Solomon's death in 922 B.C. was the occasion for the eruption of these resentments.

At his father's death Solomon's son, Rehoboam, made the mistake of heeding the advice of his young counselors rather than listening to the older, wiser men of the court. The latter suggested that he ease the people's burdens, but the young hotheads told him to talk and act tough. He did, and he lost his kingdom. All except the tribes of Judah and Benjamin successfully revolted under the leadership of Jeroboam, a former overseer under Solomon. These people established a new nation which they called Israel. Its capital was set up at the ancient religious center of the confederacy, Shechem. Its southern border was only ten miles from Jerusalem. Jeroboam built shrines for worship, at Dan in the north and at Bethel near the southern border. Golden calves were set up as symbols of worship, illustrating the idolatry which characterized Israel throughout her history.

For the next two hundred years (922–722 B.C.) Israel's fortunes fluctuated. A succession of kings, each usually more wicked than his predecessor, ruled the country. Frequent assassinations of kings compounded the instability of the government. Syria, Israel's neighbor to the northeast, continually threatened the security of the border. By overthrowing the reigning king, an able man named Omri came to power in 876 B.C. and established a stable government. Under Omri the capital was moved to Samaria, which was made into a fortress, and Israel became a formidable power. Omri was succeeded by his son, Ahab, remembered primarily because of his wife, Jezebel. This domineering woman, daughter of the king of Tyre and a zealous advocate of Baalism, sought to turn Israel to the worship of the immoral fertility cult practiced by Canaanites. Had it not been for the fearless and stout opposition of the prophet Elijah, she might have succeeded. The last strong king in Israel was Jeroboam II, who in his long reign (786–746 B.C.) brought prosperity and peace to the land. Amos and Hosea, two of Israel's great prophetic voices, were heard during this period. They prophesied the decline and doom which quickly overtook the country after the reign of Jeroboam II.

At this juncture two additional factors in the history of Israel should be noted, one political and the other religious. The political force was the rise of Assyria, located northeast of Israel and Syria in Upper Mesopotamia. Assyria took its name from the city of Asshur. From the ninth century to the fall of Assyria's capital, Nineveh, to Babylon in 612 B.C., the fortunes of Israel and Judah were continually involved with Assyrian aggression. The problem came to a climax in 732 B.C. when the Assyrian Tiglath-pileser III overran Palestine, leaving Israel desolate. Finally, in 722 B.C. Sargon destroyed Samaria, deported many of Israel's people to Assyria, replaced them with masses of foreigners, and Israel as a nation ceased to exist.

The other factor in the life of Israel-Judah was the rise of the prophetic movement. The roots of prophetism go back into the early life of the people of the covenant. The Hebrew word for prophet, *nabi*, means spokesman and was applied to the spiritual role so that the prophet was a "spokesman for God." Early prophetism was strongly associated with various forms of divining as a means of discovering God's will in a particular situation. Israel's first prophets often were roving bands of ecstatics who prophesied by trances and other bizarre manifestations.

However, as the nation matured, there began to emerge great spiritual figures who spoke out fearlessly and responsibly against evil in high places or low. These men were not so much foretellers of the future as they were forthtellers. Their primary concern was not fortune-telling, but interpretation of current issues in the light of the purpose of God. They were men of moral insight who dared to claim Israel's loyalty for a moral God. Such men were Nathan, who denounced David for his sin with Bathsheba, and Elijah, who stood like a granite boulder against the devices of Jezebel, the wicked Canaanite wife of Ahab. They were often involved in the nation's political affairs, as was the prophet Elisha in arranging for the overthrow of the House of Omri by Jehu in 842 B.C. Beginning in the middle of the eighth century B.C., certain of the prophets left their oracles in written form. Such men as Amos, Hosea, Isaiah, Micah, and Jeremiah were primarily preachers; but by God's providence we have in the Bible records of their prophecies. The life of both small sister nations was in such ways inextricably bound up with the ministry of the prophets.

And Then There Was One (722–587 B.C.)

After the fall of Samaria, Judah continued as a nation for another one hundred and thirty-five years, but with indifferent success. While Israel had enjoyed temporary peace under Jeroboam II, Judah was having a similar respite under the leadership of King Uzziah (783–742 B.C.). The year of his death was marked by Isaiah as the beginning of his prophetic work. After Uzziah, there was continual pressure from Syria and Israel during the reign of Uzziah's grandson, Ahaz (735–715 B.C.). Following the fall of Samaria, Judah had to be concerned about Assyria; and in 701 B.C. the Assyrian king, Sennacherib, besieged Jerusalem, "shutting up Hezekiah, king of Jerusalem, like a bird in a cage." Through this time of great stress, the prophet Isaiah occupied a strategic position as adviser to kings, although his advice was frequently ignored. God intervened, destroyed the Assyrian army with a mysterious plague, and Judah was spared for another hundred years.

For forty-five years (687–642 B.C.) of that century one king, Manasseh, ruled. He distinguished himself as probably the most wicked king who held either throne of Israel and Judah, even going to the extent of setting up child sacrifice to the god Molech. Shortly after his death, Judah's last good king came to the throne as a result of the assassination of his father, Amon. This king was an eight-year-old boy named Josiah (640–609 B.C.). About 626 B.C., when Josiah came of age, he began to reform the country. The event, however, that ignited the flames of religious fervor was finding a book of the law in the Temple, which was under repair. This happened in 622 B.C.; and when Josiah learned the contents of the document, he instituted sweeping reforms which included the following: centering all worship in the Temple at Jerusalem, the closing of all outlying shrines and the abolishment of all Canaanite and Assyrian worship, and a time of national renewal of commitment to the covenant. Jeremiah, an outstanding religious figure, appeared on the scene about the time of the beginning of Josiah's reforms in 626 B.C. He continued his work until after the destruction of Judah in 587 B.C. He saw the reforms as inadequate because they were only external. Jeremiah believed that there must be a "new covenant," written "upon their hearts" (Jer. 31:31–34, RSV).

As the seventh century B.C. drew toward a close, the world power looming on the horizon was neo-Babylonia, the Chaldean Empire. Moving westward it challenged declining Assyria. Nineveh fell in 612 B.C., when the Assyrians suffered a crushing defeat. Pharaoh Necho of Egypt, out of no love for Assyria but in the hope of halting Babylonian expansion, marched north across Palestine to join forces with the defeated Assyrians. King Josiah of Judah foolishly sought to repulse the Egyptian army and was slain in battle at Megiddo in 609 B.C. Josiah's army was scattered and his body was returned to Jerusalem amid the shattered hopes and dreams of his people to whom he was a great hero. But the tides of history had moved past Assyria; and at Carchemish, along the upper Euphrates River in 605 B.C., the combined forces of Assyria and Egypt were decisively defeated by

Babylonian forces led by Nebuchadnezzar. Assyria and Egypt were no longer powers, and little Judah stood unprotected against Babylonian onslaughts.

The closing years of Judah's national life were difficult ones filled with uncertainty and intrigue. Jeremiah counseled cooperation with Babylon and got rebuke, rejection, beating, imprisonment, and threat of death for his payment. In 597 B.C. after a revolt by King Jehoiakim against Babylon, Judah was invaded and a considerable number of her leading citizens deported, including King Jehoiachin who had just come to the throne after his father's death. Ten years later, after another revolt, Jerusalem was besieged, captured, and destroyed. Proud Jerusalem lay in ruins, her Temple gone and her walls leveled. Zedekiah, the puppet who had led the revolt, had his eyes put out after being forced to watch his sons executed, and another deportation of a large number of citizens took place. So ended Judah's hope that the house of David would occupy the throne forever.

Exile and Restoration

The biblical material dealing with this period is found in Ezra and Nehemiah, the prophetic works of Ezekiel and Isaiah 40–66, and some of the psalms. Babylonian and Persian records are also helpful in trying to trace the history of this time. In Babylon the Hebrew exiles were treated well. They lived in a colony to themselves along the Chebar River. Many prospered, engaging in the business and professional life of the Chaldeans. In fact, Babylonian records of leading merchants of the city include Jewish names, indicating that some of them chose to remain in Babylon after the captivity ended.

In other ways Babylon influenced the people of the covenant. They began to use Aramaic as their spoken language. Their horizon was widened as they were exposed to another culture. But most of all, certain new emphases emerged in their religion. No longer was the Temple available as the center of religious life. Other means of maintaining loyalty to God had to be developed. Some of the religious results were the appearance of the synagogue, stricter observance of sabbath and other ceremonial regulations, the study of the Scriptures, and the development of a theological basis for understanding the tragedy of the Exile. Separated from Jerusalem and the Temple, Judaism as a system of religion began to emerge. The scribe, so influential in Jesus' day, began to be a force in Hebrew religious life as he sought to preserve and interpret the faith of his fathers.

Meanwhile, back in Judah life had not ceased to exist, although it was disorganized and spiritless. Clans from the Negeb probably moved up into the country, as did Samaritans move down into it; and a mixed population began to develop, bringing a mixture of religion with it.

In 539 B.C. Babylon fell to a new conqueror, Cyrus of Persia. One of his first decrees was an edict permitting the Jews to return to Judah; and in 538 B.C., a group set out for Jerusalem. The anticipation was greater than the achievement. When they got to Jerusalem, they found the city still in ruins after the passage of fifty years; and they also found that those who had remained were suspicious and hostile. Moreover, there was constant threat from surrounding peoples who viewed with something less than enthusiasm the prospect of Jerusalem's being rebuilt. So dispirited were the returnees that eighteen years passed before the work of rebuilding the Temple began. Finally, with the urging of the prophets Haggai and Zechariah, the construction of the new Temple got under way in 520 B.C. under the direction of Zerubbabel and was completed four years later. This second Temple was not to be compared with Solomon's, but it did at least provide a symbol for the rallying of all Israel to the faith. Zerubbabel's Temple was not replaced until the time of Herod the Great near the date of the birth of Jesus.

Morale in Judah did not rise appreciably even after the completion of the Temple. The nature and extent of the problems is the subject of Malachi, the last writing appearing in our Old Testament. Malachi wrote about callousness in worship, the prevalence of divorce, and withholding of tithes, the offering of inferior animals in sacrifice, and the low moral life of priest and people alike. Into this situation came Nehemiah and Ezra, two of the most important Jewish men in Israel's late history.

Nehemiah was an official of the Persian king in Babylon; but, learning of the low estate of affairs in his homeland, he petitioned for and received permission to go to Judah. Arriving about 440 B.C., he found the walls of the city still unbuilt and the morale low. Immediately, he set about to organize a task force and complete the work. Within two years he had fortified the city and made it secure against its enemies. Having completed the task of providing adequate defense, Nehemiah next turned to internal reforms. In this work he was assisted by a priest named Ezra whose emphasis upon teaching and interpreting the Torah (law), upon the synagogue, and the purification of worship practices has caused many to refer to him as "the father of Judaism." The work of Nehemiah, the politician, and Ezra, the priest, was one of identifying nationalism and religion as representing a single cause. This identification was a major factor in Jewish survival of the efforts of the Greeks to Hellenize the world.

The people of the covenant could not be immune to events of world history. When, therefore, in 331 B.C., the Persian Empire was destroyed by the armies of a young military genius named Alexander the Great, the impact upon the Jewish nation was immeasurable. Alexander was fired by more than the desire for military conquest. He had been a pupil of the Greek philosopher, Aristotle; and it was his ambition to press upon all the world Greek ideas, language, and culture. Greek colonies began to dot the east—Alexandria in Egypt, Antioch in Syria, Sebaste (Samaria) in Palestine. Greek theaters and gymnasiums were built in major cities where youth could be imbued with Greek culture.

Could the exclusiveness of the Jewish faith survive? That was an open question at the end of what might be termed "The Old Testament Era." For although Alexander died, 323 B.C., before his cultural revolution had more than begun, it continued to be the major problem of Jewish religious life for the next three hundred years.

CHAPTER FIVE

How the
Old Testament
Came to Be

The Torah

After a sketchy panoramic view of Old Testament history, it will be helpful now to see when and how the parts of it came together. With reverent honesty, we must admit what we do not know and carefully distinguish between speculation and fact. The first five books of the Old Testament, known in Hebrew as Torah (law), were written about a period of indeterminate length, from creation to the close of the wilderness wandering of Israel, about 1250 B.C.*

Genesis is appropriately named, the title being taken from the opening Hebrew word, meaning "in beginning." This book is about beginning. "In the beginning God created" is its foundational and overarching affirmation. The first eleven chapters are essentially great confessions of faith which account for the realities of our human life and religious experience. These chapters are about the primeval ages of man and are not written from the scientific point of view. It is idle to try to fit them into the timetables of astronomy, anthropology,

*Editor's Note: Dates and authorship of Old Testament books are difficult to determine. The discussions in this chapter are based upon the author's lifetime of study, but the conclusions arrived at here are not undisputed by other scholars. Such matters will be dealt with more fully in subsequent survey volumes.

geology, biology, and a half dozen other scientific disciplines. The truth of which the narratives are vehicles is the eternal Word of God.

Here the great questions that have always stirred the hearts of men are answered with a resounding affirmation of faith in a personal Creator who is both righteous and loving and who has made man for fellowship with God and with his brothers. Here are pictured our repeated human sin and folly and their consequences. With uncommon beauty and clarity the vagaries of human life are exposed, along with the unvarying purpose of God to bring redemption through a Chosen People to the race which he created.

The creation account (told in two forms: Gen. 1:1 to 2:4a and Gen. 2:4b–25) is full of symbolic rather than scientific meaning. "Adam" means man or the first man. "Eden" is a Hebrew word meaning enchantment, or delight; the root word translated "Eve" means life or living. Man is created in God's image; that is, he is unique in the order of creation, made to have communion with his Creator. He is made not only for fellowship but also for self-development and for mastery of the rest of creation. But man, made for mastery of the creation as God's agent, does not wish to be an agent. He wishes to be master. As the creation account answers the question, How did we get here?, the story of the fall answers the timeless question, Why is evil so persistent? Why can't we do right?

As the fact of sin is awesome, so are its consequences. Sin brings separation between the Creator and sinful man who, now ashamed and afraid, hides. It brings disorder to man's relationship with the rest of creation; now he must "wrestle" with the earth to earn his bread. Finally, sin brings death, as man is excluded from the Garden and, knowing his mortality, wistfully longs for Eden. But there is ultimate victory over sin; the serpent's head will be bruised by the seed of woman.

Sin's consequences also affect the generations. The story of Cain and Abel (Gen. 4) affirms a timeless truth about human relationships. We devour and destroy one another. But God will not be defeated. Cain may slay Abel and prove himself unfit, but God will raise up a Seth through whom the promise may continue. Sin is not only a personal matter, however, but also a problem of society. The Flood (Gen. 6–9) illustrates the universal extent of evil and God's judgment upon it. "The Lord saw that the wickedness of man was great in the earth, and that every imagination of the thoughts of his heart was only evil continually" (Gen. 6:5, RSV). The fact that the Genesis account of the Flood shares a tradition common to the ancient world about a great deluge need not be a source of embarrassment to be explained away. It is a fact, and the visitor to the British Museum may be shown a clay tablet from seventh-century Nineveh telling the Babylonian *Gilgamesh Epic* of a huge flood that inundated the earth. The uniqueness of the Genesis account is its understanding of the meaning of the event. It sees the Flood as the working out of the purpose of a righteous God who has created man for righteous fellowship with himself and who makes a new beginning with man after the deluge. The rainbow is a sign of hope, a form of covenant between a faithful God and penitent man.

But the testimony of Genesis is that man is unable and unwilling to keep faith. His overweening pride always asserts itself to declare independence of God. This is the meaning of the Tower of Babel. Historical event is used to teach a basic truth. Babel is Babylon, a city whose brick step-pyramids, called ziggurats, must have been an awesome sight to the Semitic nomad from the flat desert pressing in upon the fringes of civilization. To a wanderer used to the open country, the city of Babylon would be the epitome of human pride, arrogance, and evil. Here was gathered up all that man could do with his own ingenuity. It symbolized prideful rebellion against God. Man seeks to build his own order; he is forever constructing a Tower of Babel to penetrate the utmost reaches of God's heaven. But it is a foolish impertinence. God scatters what sinful pride gathers.

As we turn to chapter 12 of Genesis, we realize that we are dealing with a different form of truth. Genesis 1–11 has telescoped ages whose time is known only to God. When we come to Abraham, however, we know where we are—the beginning of the second millennium B.C. in the Mesopotamian cradle of civilization at a time of Semitic migration. Genesis records the selection and guidance of the people of God by tracing the pilgrimage of a faithful man, Abraham, and his family into Canaan and down to Egypt. The remainder of Genesis is devoted to the story of God's preparation of his people to become the nation Israel.

Exodus unfolds the drama of God's emancipation of his people from Egypt and records their first step toward becoming a nation. God is seen as the Leader who uses his servant, Moses, to free the people and bring them to Sinai where the law is given. The law is more than a series of general principles embodied in the Ten Commandments. Exodus 20; 34; and Deuteronomy 5 all contain statements of this Decalogue, the first four clarifying specific obligations toward God and the last six dealing with responsibility toward one's fellowman. But these fundamental principles were elaborated in the covenant code, found in Exodus 20:22 to 23:33, in which practical applications were made of each of the Ten Commandments to specific situations in everyday life.

Israel's religion was expressed not only in terms of beliefs and ethical requirements, but also in terms of its forms of worship. These forms are given in explicit detail in the latter part of Exodus (chaps. 25–31; 35–40) and in certain parts of the book of Leviticus (chaps. 1–7; 23). Most of the rest of Leviticus, so named because the Levites were designated as priests and administrators of the ritual law, is taken up with instructions of what is permissible and forbidden in the daily life of the people. All of life had a religious orientation and every act was significant in terms of faithfulness or unfaithfulness.

Events taking place in the wilderness around Kadesh-barnea before the beginning of the invasion of Canaan under Joshua are recorded in the book of Numbers. The book was known to the Israelites by a Hebrew word meaning "in the wilderness." In the second century B.C., the Septuagint (a Greek translation of the Old Testament) named it "Numbers" because it opens with a census of the people of Israel. From the Septuagint to Jerome's Latin Vulgate to our English translations the title Numbers has come, but it is a misnomer. Numbers is an account of the trials and difficulties of a wandering people being transformed into a nation. It closes with descriptions of the settlement of some of the people of Israel east of the Jordan, indicating that the conquest did not involve the land of Canaan alone.

The book of Deuteronomy, as were the other books of the Torah, was known by its opening words, "these are the words" (RSV), or "the words." As in the case of Numbers, however, the Septuagint translators renamed the work, calling it "second law." It is a summary of Israel's religion written for public proclamation. It is likely that the form of the law read to the people on occasions of a national renewal of the covenant was Deuteronomy. In 621 B.C., during the reign of King Josiah in Judah, a copy of the law was discovered and brought to the king who, having heard its provisions, instituted national reform. This could have been Deuteronomy. Scarcely any book of the Old Testament is more frequently quoted in the New, more than eighty times in all. The reason is evident. Deuteronomy embodies an exalted résumé of God's election of Israel, his covenant with her, and his expectations of her. Three addresses (sermons) contain this material. The first (1:6 to 4:40) recounts God's works with his people and calls them to obedience. The second is the longest and makes up the main body of the book (5:1 to 28:68). It is a summary of God's law. The third sermon (29–30) is an exhortation to keep the covenant and offers the alternatives of life or death as results of obedience or disobedience. The writing concludes with an account of Moses' death.

Historical Narratives

The book of Joshua deals with the era of the conquest of Canaan, about fifty years. If one continues to turn the pages of the Old Testament, the very next book is Judges, which is about the period of the confederation of Israel's tribes, lasting some two hundred years until the beginning of the monarchy in 1020 B.C.

Passing by the book of Ruth, a charming story about the days of the confederation but written from a later period and perspective of Israel's history, we come to the book of 1 Samuel. It is something of a transitional work (as Samuel was a transitional figure) between the time of tribalism and Judges in Israel, to the time of the monarchy and the prophets. The first nine chapters of 1 Samuel lead up to the anointing of Saul as Israel's first king by Samuel, while the remainder of the first book recounts the reign of King Saul, concluding with his death on Mount Gilboa by his own hand.

Samuel's attitudes toward Saul were somewhat ambivalent as seen in 1 Samuel; and long before Saul's untimely end the aged Samuel had anointed his successor, the shepherd lad, David. All of 2 Samuel and the first two chapters of 1 Kings record the glorious reign of King David. The story of King Solomon, David's son and successor, will be found in 1 Kings 1–11. (Chaps. 1–2 record the struggle between Solomon and another son, Adonijah, for the throne at the end of David's life.) At the death of Solomon, his son, Rehoboam, found himself unable to cope with the spirit of revolt that had been building up during the oppressive reign of his father. Rehoboam lost all save Judah and Benjamin in the south to Jeroboam. The latter became the first king of the nation in the north which took the name "Israel."

From 1 Kings 12 through 2 Kings 18 the story of two centuries
(922–722 B.C.) of intrigue, war, evil, and punishment from God is
interwoven with the two strands of history—the kings of Judah and
the kings of Israel. The record is put together with a definite pattern.
In introducing each of the kings of Israel, four historical matters are
mentioned: the dating of the beginning of the king's reign in terms of
the corresponding king of Judah; the name of the capital; the dura-
tion of the reign; and a short summary condemning the king for doing
evil in the sight of God. Also, in reporting the reigns of the kings of
Judah, four facts are always mentioned: the date of accession as related to Israel's king; the age of the monarch when he came to the
throne; his mother's name; and a brief comparison of the king with
David. The story goes back and forth from one nation to the other
until Israel was destroyed by the Assyrians in 722 B.C. The remainder
of 2 Kings records the history of Judah from 722 B.C. until her fall to
Babylon in 587 B.C.

Turn the pages on to the Chronicles. Much of this material deals
with the same period reviewed in the Samuel-Kings books. It will also
be noted that Chronicles begins with a genealogy of the people of
Israel by tribes, and that the history is being reviewed from a time
after the exile to Babylon (1 Chron. 9:1). If the Samuel-Kings history and the Chronicles were placed in parallel columns according to
subject matter, some interesting relationships would be revealed.
For one thing, the Chronicler evidently had access to the Samuel-
Kings material and drew upon it, sometimes even excerpting passages
word for word. (This would not be regarded by an ancient as in any
way unbecoming, for they did not have our ideas of plagiarism.)
Further, we would notice that the Chronicler, writing long after the
Northern Kingdom of Israel had fallen, had little interest in that history but wrote from a perspective of Judah. We would also see that
he emphasized the religious rather than the political aspects of David's
career. The reason for this is that the Chronicler, who was also
probably responsible for the books of Ezra and Nehemiah, was writing
from the perspective of postexilic Hebrew faith. He was an interpreter of history, rather than a reporter, and therefore chose those
aspects of his people's past which related to his convictions concerning
God's intentions for the restored nation under the guidance of the
priests after the Exile.

With the books of Ezra and Nehemiah, the historical survey of the

Old Testament is complete. These two books report the conditions existing in postexilic Judaism. The period about which they are concerned is the fifth century B.C. As we shall see, we have some writings in the Old Testament that come from later times and are concerned with later situations; but there are no histories of subsequent periods in the Old Testament canon.

Many Authors But One Source

We can say with confident faith that God is the source of the inspired biblical writings without impoverishing the rich variety of authorship of the Scriptures. The people of Israel had a long history before anyone ever wrote any of it down. How was that history preserved and passed on from generation to generation? It was embedded in the very marrow of Israel's being. It was the priceless heritage of a father to his children and his children's children. God had done mighty things for his people. Nothing was so important as the preservation and transmission of that history. This was the manner in which it was done before it was written.

But what about Moses? Did he not write the first five books? It would be next to impossible to draw the figure of Moses greater than it was in Israel's history. He received the law from God. Israel and all who are the new Israel in Christ look to him as the human source of the law which underlay and defined the life of the people of God. As Elijah represented the prophetic voice, so Moses personified the law. It was fitting that on the mount of transfiguration, Moses and Elijah should be seen with Jesus, for they embodied the major religious concepts of Israel—law and prophets. It was quite understandable that Jesus should say, "Did not Moses give you the law?" (John 7:19). He was the one through whom the law came.

It is an oversimplification, however, to think of Moses as sitting down and writing the first five books of the Old Testament as they appear in the Bible. Perhaps the best way to visualize the role of Moses in the law is to think of him as the human agent responsible for the basic precepts and underlying principles given at Sinai. Much of the law reflects periods after Moses, and was gradually accumulated as new circumstances demanded the making of additional applications of the basic law. The principle here is similar to that which causes us in the United States to speak of all law as "constitutional law." We mean that all our laws are based upon the Constitution even though they might have been enacted many years after the Constitution came into being. It is important that we never assume that the inspiration of a book in the Bible is dependent on the book's having only one author or having been written all at one time. These considerations are not necessary to our understanding of inspiration.

Further, when we examine these first five books of the Bible and the other books that record the historical narrative of Israel until after the restoration from exile, we are led to feel that these are not the products of a single hand. They are more nearly collections of several separate records of the same events, and they come from different groups in Israel's life. Moreover, before they were written records, they were oral accounts of things that had happened. Gathered into great sagas of history to be recited in the home or at a religious festival, these oral accounts were passed along from one generation to another as priceless heritages until God directed that they be put in written form.

No one can be positive about it, but there appear to have been several separate accounts of the historical narratives of Israel which were worked into a composite story in the Bible. It is like having several people prepare separate accounts of the same happening and then having someone take all the reports and put them together. These accounts are like strands of a rope, except that the strands do not all begin at the same place or end together. They overlap and intertwine, supplementing one another and adding to the total perspective of historical event and Israel's faith concerning God. Some deal with the history of the eras covered, some with regulations for worship, and some with ethical demands. The materials appear to have been written over a long period of time stretching from the era of King Solomon until after the return from the Babylonian exile, at which time the various strands were woven into a composite history of God's people from creation to restoration.

The Golden Age of Prophecy

Prophecy lies deep in Israel's history, antedating by centuries the first writing prophets of the Bible. One has but to recall the names of Nathan, Micaiah, Elijah, and Elisha to be reminded that "spokesmen for God" were familiar figures. Their prophetic powers were regarded as a gift from God, and they often wielded a large influence over national policy. Elijah, for example, waged a courageous and relentless war against Baalism in Israel and was regarded by Queen Jezebel as her most formidable foe. Prophets were not simply lone "voices crying in the wilderness."

In the middle of the eighth century B.C., one of those remarkable periods occurred when an uncommonly large number of outstanding people appeared at one time. There came on the scene four great prophets, two in Israel and two in Judah, each of whom left a legacy of written oracles later embodied in the Scriptures. The first of these was Amos, native of Tekoa, a village in the hills of Judah. Amos came to preach at Bethel, one of the two religious centers of Israel. There against the thinly-veiled warning of the priest in charge, Amaziah, he prophesied. His message rang with righteous indignation at the sins of a nation which allowed some to wallow in self-indulgent luxury while others experienced the direst poverty. His charges were specific: oppression of the poor, inequity in the courts, luxury in the midst of want, gross immorality, and arrogant pride. In a series of five visions, Amos described the judgment of God upon a nation which was heedless of righteousness.

The second of these prophets was Hosea, a contemporary of Amos. He looked upon the same conditions, but his response was prompted by another understanding of God. He saw God as grieving, loving Israel and forgiving her obstinate sinfulness. Using the tragedy of his own broken marriage, the profligacy of his wife Gomer, as an example of Israel's violation of covenant relationship with God, Hosea wrote with unforgettable and touching tenderness of God's unswerving devotion to his people.

While Amos and Hosea were prophesying in Israel, Isaiah was a prophet in Judah. Possibly of the royal household, he has been called "prince of prophets." He dated his prophetic work from "the year that king Uzziah died" (Isa. 6:1), which was about 742 B.C. During much of his career, Isaiah sought to get Judah's king to rely upon God and not get involved in entangling alliances with foreign powers. His visions of the greatness and holiness of God are recorded in some of the most majestic passages of the Bible. His messianic expectation, reflected in such chapters as Isaiah 7, 9, and 11, illustrate for Christians the major theme of redemption running throughout the Bible. Many scholars see the prophecies of Isaiah of Judah in the eighth century as coming to a close at the end of chapter 39. The latter part of the book which bears Isaiah's name (chaps. 40–66) was written of the exile to Babylon which occurred more than a century later.

The last of the four great eighth-century prophets was Micah, probably a tradesman in a village close to Jerusalem. The message of Micah throbs with concern for the "little man," victimized by wealthy absentee landowners and other powerful figures who usurp his rights and "tear the skin off" his body (3:1-3, RSV). Micah's resounding theme was doom for Judah because of her moral decay. But he had glimpses of that far-off day of peace when "they shall sit every man under his vine and under his fig tree, and none shall make them afraid" (4:4, RSV).

Prophets of the Doom of Jerusalem

After the fall of Samaria in 722 B.C., prophecy ceased in Israel; but prophetic writing continued to come out of Judah in the seventh century and up to the end of the Southern Kingdom in 587 B.C. Among these were Zephaniah, Nahum, Habakkuk, and Jeremiah.

The chief historical value of the book of Zephaniah is its picture of the moral decay of Judah that took place during the long reign of Manasseh (687–642 B.C.). He cited such evils as the adoption of foreign customs (1:8–9); the assumption that God was irrelevant (1:12); and the violence, fraud, idolatry, pride, and corruption which prevailed (3:3–4).

The book of Nahum is one of the most dramatic and dreadful descriptions of the terror of war in all literature. It is written of the destruction of Nineveh, proud capital of Assyria, in 612 B.C. by the Babylonians. Assyria, scourge of little countries for more than a century, had now received double for all her sins. And the prophet rejoiced at her humiliation and suffering. Curiously, Nahum means "comfort"!

Habakkuk belongs to this same period at the close of the seventh century, the time of the decline of Assyria and the rise of Babylon. This prophet raised moral questions about how Judah could stand when she was so wicked. He got no comfort from the thought that Judah would fall to Babylon, for the prophet knew that Babylon was even more godless than his own people. The prophecy closes with a testimony of faith in God's trustworthiness (3:17–19).

In some ways Jeremiah may be the greatest prophet of the Old Testament. He is certainly the one about whom we know most, for his prophecies are filled with self-revealing passages reflecting a sensitive nature, an uncommon capacity for concern, a deep passion for his nation, and a staunch faith in God. Beginning his career during the early days of King Josiah, Jeremiah watched the nation come through the reforms instituted in 621 B.C., perhaps favoring them at first, only to realize afterward that they were external and inadequate to save Judah from decline.

Jeremiah's destiny was to oppose the trends of his day. He became a harsh critic of national policy, believing that it would lead to disaster. He was at odds with the times, with his king, with other prophets, and with the people generally. His life was often in danger; he was threatened, beaten, imprisoned, scoffed at, and called an enemy of his country which he loved with all his being. Sometimes he felt he could not go on, and bewailed his lot, regretting that he had been born or that he had not died at birth.

Jeremiah was a man with a dramatic flair. On one occasion he made a public demonstration of his faith in the future of the country by purchasing a field from a relative at the very moment the Babylonians were besieging Jerusalem. He had the deed of purchase carefully recorded, because he said: " 'Thus says the Lord of hosts, the God of Israel: Houses and fields and vineyards shall again be bought in this land' " (Jer. 32:15, RSV).

When Jerusalem was overrun by the Babylonians, first in 597 and again in 587 B.C., and large numbers of her leading people taken captive to Babylon, Jeremiah chose to remain with those left. From Jerusalem he wrote a letter of courage and hope to the exiles admonishing them to "seek the welfare of the city" and believe in God who planned "to give you a future and a hope" (29:11, RSV). Later the aged prophet, kidnapped by a group of rebels against the Babylonians, was carried to Egypt where he must have died.

It is impossible to measure the stature of this man. If one were to point to his greatest single contribution to the religion of Israel, it would probably be his concept of the new covenant which God would some day give his people. It would be an inner, spiritual covenant: "I will put my law within them, and I will write it upon their hearts" (31:33, RSV).

Prophets of the Exile and Restoration

Two other prophets of the Old Testament may be mentioned briefly as belonging to the period of the Exile (597–538 B.C.). One is

Ezekiel, a priest in Jerusalem whose prophetic work began before the Exile and continued over into it after he was transported to Babylon, possibly in the first deportation of 597 B.C. A contemporary of Jeremiah, he was a visionary, a religious eccentric, whose prophecies border on the ecstatic. He engaged in acted parables, sometimes bizarre acts, in order to illustrate a prophetic conviction. The first part of his prophecy is doom and judgment. Once, however, Judah had fallen, Ezekiel became a prophet of hope. Perhaps the most familiar example of the prophecy of hope is the vision of "dry bones" which God made to live again (Ezek. 37).

The other great prophetic writing of the Exile appears in chapters 40–66 of the book of Isaiah. Many scholars call the author Deutero-Isaiah, "Second Isaiah." These prophecies resound with the hope of salvation. The Lord of history, who had brought his people from Egypt to Canaan and then to Babylon, would restore them and bless them. But perhaps even more important than his understanding of history as the arena of God's activity was this prophet's great insight into the nature of redemption as coming through suffering. Four beautiful poems, called the Servant Songs, appear in this prophecy: Isaiah 42:1–4; 49:1–6; 50:4–9; 52:13 to 53:12. Christians who read these poems cannot help seeing them as accurate and exalted descriptions of Christ.

After the return from the Exile, other prophets spoke and wrote in an effort to prod the people to get on with the work of rebuilding the Temple. One such man was the prophet Haggai, whose book contains five prophecies all dating in the year 520 B.C., and all soundly denouncing the people for failure to reconstruct the Temple. " 'Why? says the Lord of hosts. Because of my house that lies in ruins, while you busy yourselves each with his own house' " (1:9, RSV). Further, he promised that if they would build the Lord's house, prosperity would return to the nation: " 'In this place I will give prosperity' " (2:9, RSV).

Another of these postexilic prophets was Zechariah, in whose fourteen chapters appear the notes of appeal to repentance and obedience to God. A third, Joel, is perhaps best known to Christians for the passage which Peter quoted on the day of Pentecost to show that the coming of the Holy Spirit was the fulfilment of prophecy (Joel 2:28).

The next seventy-five years following the completion of the second Temple in 516 B.C. remain obscure. Conditions in Judea were not much improved. Nearly a century had passed since the first exiles had returned from Babylon, and the walls of Jerusalem had not yet been built. Then Nehemiah, a prominent Jew in Babylon, arrived in 440 B.C., armed with authority from King Artaxerxes I to direct the rebuilding of the walls. Obadiah, the shortest book of the Old Testament, is a prophecy which reflects this general lack of morale. It gives vent to bitter hatred of the Edomites for taking advantage of Judah during her time of distress at Jerusalem's fall.

Another and better known prophecy is Malachi. This writing reflects the low moral ebb of Judah and denounces both priest and people for their careless indifference toward such duties as worship, the payment of tithes, respect for marriage vows, and the responsibility of brotherliness. The prophecy of Malachi reflects a device which is familiar in teaching. There is an assertion which is said to be the declaration of God. Then there is the people's reply to that assertion in the form of a question which asks, "In what way is this true?" This question then gives rise to a second declaration which in turn calls forth another question, providing occasion for another answer, and so on. When we come to Malachi, it is evident that we have come near the end of the great era of prophets of Israel.

Prophetic and Other Writings of the Greek Period

From the time of Alexander the Great (died 323 B.C.), Judaism struggled against the encroachments of Greek culture. Since the restoration, Jewish religion had become more and more priest-oriented with emphasis upon ritual observance. The Pharisees, with their devotion to the law, had not yet arisen; but the seeds of Pharisaism were present in the growth of the synagogue and the teaching of the law.

The setting of the book of Daniel is the Exile. That is when Daniel lived, according to information in the book itself. However, a widely held view is that when persecution became fierce during the oppression by the Greeks and the revolt of the Maccabeans (168–165 B.C.), this unusual apocalyptic work appeared. This book was placed among the Writings, the last works to receive canonical status, in the Hebrew Bible. Although Daniel's setting was a scene from the earlier time of the Exile, this latter view holds that the book of Daniel came from the days of Jewish struggle for religious freedom. Using familiar stories of the heroism of a brave young Hebrew who had successfully resisted Babylonian efforts to corrupt him, even though his life was in danger, the writer of Daniel appealed to his fellow countrymen to exercise similar courage, perseverance, and faith, even unto death. Whether one sees this prophecy as the work of a prophet of the Exile or of the Greek period, the book of Daniel has the marks of apocalyptic literature—cryptic language, hidden meanings, eschatalogical hope in God's ultimate victory—and is the chief example of such writing in the Old Testament. It is important to our understanding of the total revelation of God.

Esther is another late Old Testament book which makes a strong appeal for fidelity in the face of trial. This writing is ardently nationalistic, telling how a Jewish girl named Esther was able to foil the evil purposes of a wicked prime minister to the Persian king, Xerxes I (486–465 B.C.), whose wife she had become. This book is generally believed to have been written in the Maccabean period when Jewish nationalism was intense.

The books of Ruth and Jonah emphasize the opposite point of view. Ruth is a charming story set back in the period of the Judges and is designed to produce a less narrow spirit of racial and national pride. Ruth was a foreigner, of the Moabites, for whom Jews had little respect. She married a Jew, accepted the faith of the Jews, and became one of the ancestors of King David. One could not have better credentials.

The book of Jonah is even bolder in its proclamation of God's concern for the non-Jew. Like several other Old Testament books, its setting is likely an earlier period than the one in which it was written. It is set in the eighth century, but its message is timeless, saying with unmistakable clarity that God is concerned for the salvation of the foreigner, even the despised oppressor like the Assyrian, just as he is concerned for the salvation of Israel. These two, Ruth and Jonah, came as great missionary messages in an age of drawing in and of exclusiveness.

One other form of biblical writing, most of it done in this late Greek-Maccabean period, is Wisdom Literature, a type of writing which deals with the great issues of life's meaning and the employment of one's time and abilities so as to obtain the good life. It is the closest thing in the Old Testament to philosophy. Wisdom Literature was not peculiar to Israel; indeed it did not mainly appear in Israel, but throughout the Near East and particularly in Egypt. Nor did Wisdom Literature date only from the late Hellenistic period of Judaism, but it went back to the time of Solomon, whose wisdom was celebrated widely. But Wisdom Literature flourished during the post-exilic period, reflecting Persian and Greek influences on Hebrew thought. There are three notable examples of such writing in the Old Testament: Proverbs, Ecclesiastes, and Job.

Proverbs is a collection covering a great span of years from Solomon in the tenth century to the Hellenistic period. Its chief message is how to live a good and successful life.

Ecclesiastes, whose title is actually "The Preacher," is a melancholy and skeptical commentary on the futility of life: Nothing matters, neither pleasure nor piety, neither work nor play, neither plenty nor fame. All is vanity; virtue is not rewarded, nor is wickedness punished. "As is the good man, so is the sinner" (9:2, RSV). One should be wise and remain uninvolved, for people who get caught up in causes are likely to be hurt and "a living dog is better than a dead lion" (9:4, RSV). All things come to the same end; life is boringly repetitious, and all is vanity. One should remember the Creator in the days of one's youth before the infirmities of old age assail the body and reduce it to a tremulous and pitiable shell. Such seems to be the tone of the book. One writer has summarized the book thus: "Ecclesiastes is a wisdom book in which the writer seeks to discover what is good for man to do during the few days of his life." [1]

Job is a drama of amazing skill and depth, raising profound questions about the nature of man and God and the meaning of human suffering. The drama opens with a prologue in which the proposition is put that Job represents the finest of the human species, but that it must yet be determined whether his goodness is only his way of "paying God back" for prosperity and happiness. Withdraw these blessings and see whether he will continue to honor God and live uprightly. Job is then reduced to extremity. As once he epitomized health, wealth, and happiness, now he epitomizes utter calamity. The drama proper then unfolds, using the device of friends who represent popular religious perspectives and who assure Job that God is eager to forgive and restore him to his former estate if he will only repent of his sin. He continues to protest loudly and vehemently that he is an innocent sufferer. The writer makes a devastating attack upon the idea that suffering is always prima facie evidence of having sinned against God, and, upon its equally vicious corollary, that goodness will always be favored with prosperity and health. But the most profound message of Job concerns man's need to know God personally.

Such personal experience can come only, said the writer of Job, from man's realization of his utter need and total dependency.

The Psalms

One last group of Old Testament writings should be observed. This is the "hymnbook" of Judaism, the psalms, a collection of Hebrew poetry which covers many centuries, themes, and situations. Actually, the book of Psalms is an anthology of one hundred and fifty poems representative of every period of Israelite history. During the postexilic period, Psalms was arbitrarily divided into five sections: 1–41; 42–72; 73–89; 90–106; and 107–150. But the divisions have nothing to do with their classifications. Some are hymns for public and private worship, others are laments (either personal or corporate), while others are songs of thanksgiving, and still others are songs to be used by royalty.

Not all of the psalms of the Old Testament appear in this book, which indicates the importance of psalmody in the Hebrew religion and that the psalter is only a selective or representative anthology. The psalms are ascribed to various persons, including David, Asaph, Moses, and the sons of Korah (apparently a guild of Temple choir members), and they are written about almost every condition of life. One remembers great psalms that have spoken to one's own spiritual condition: Psalms 1; 23; 32; 42; 51; 90; 91; 100; 103; 137; 139. Perhaps each reader will have his own particular favorite psalm, and the very fact that this is true witnesses to the profound depth of spiritual meaning in these timeless songs of Israel.

In this chapter we have thumbed through the Old Testament from the literary perspective. We have been examining the times and occasions of their authorship and have sought to place them in the larger framework of the biblical revelation. It is to be hoped that the reader will feel himself somewhat less a stranger to the books of the Old Testament than before, and that the "thumbing through" survey method used here will cause him to have a greater appreciation of each of these separate works, as well as of the Old Testament itself. We shall have failed in our purpose, however, if there has not been communicated through this chapter the reverent conviction that God has indeed spoken his word through these words of Scripture.

---

[1] Edgar V. McKnight, *Opening the Bible* (Nashville: Broadman Press, 1968), p. 63.

CHAPTER SIX

Places and People of the New Testament

Part I—The Coming of Christ

It has been claimed that everything begins with the Greeks. Whether or not that is a justifiable generalization, it is where we begin New Testament study. This presumes, of course, an understanding that the roots of our faith are in the Old Testament, and one does not sever the roots from the tree. The legacy of Alexander the Great was the serious attempt to create a one-world Greek culture. Jewish resistance to Hellenism is the climate in which the Judaism of Jesus' time emerged and in which Christianity began. So we now pick up the thread of places and people, and we do so at the point of the death of Alexander the Great, 323 B.C.

The Maccabean Revolt

For a hundred and fifty years after the death of Alexander the Great, Palestine was again the battleground for two great powers, the Ptolemies of Egypt and the Seleucids of Syria. Having inherited portions of Alexander's empire, they fought each other over control of Palestine. In addition to military and political burdens first from one and then from the other, Jews of Palestine were continually under pressure to accept Greek ideas and ideals. After 198 B.C., the Seleucids achieved decisive control, resulting in more intense efforts to Hellenize the Jews.

In 168 B.C., matters reached a breaking point. Antiochus IV, who called himself Epiphanes ("Illustrious"), threatened by the encroachments of the now-powerful Roman Empire, sought to unite his provinces by strictly enforcing the claims of Hellenism. The Jews resisted all the more strenuously, and Antiochus responded by sending his army into Jerusalem. Her fortifications were destroyed, the city looted, the Temple ransacked, many inhabitants slaughtered, and the worship of God halted. The worst of all indignities was the erection in the Temple of an altar to Zeus and the offering of swine upon it. Sacrifices to the Olympian deities were made compulsory throughout the land, and the practice of Judaism forbidden under penalty of death.

Although the situation appeared desperate, relief was forthcoming. In the mountain village of Modin, an aged priest named Mattathias and his five sons struck the spark that lighted the fires of resistance. They slew a Greek officer who came to their village to enforce the compulsory sacrifice and executed the Jew who was participating in it. Then they fled to the hills, calling all who would join the resistance. Mattathias soon died; and one of his sons, Judas, called Maccabaeus, the "Hammerer," became the leader. An effective guerrilla warfare was carried on with widespread support from the Jewish population, including a conservative group called Hasidim, "Pious Ones," who regarded any compromise with Hellenism as apostasy. The guerrilla forces of Judas harassed and defeated the Seleucids in one engagement after another until they won the restoration of religious freedom. In 165 B.C., the Temple was rededicated to God in a ceremony which was kept annually thereafter as the Feast of Dedication, or Lights, and is known today as Hanukkah.

But political freedom was still to be won and with the restoration of religious liberty many Jews, including the Hasidim, withdrew their support of the revolt. Judas and his band fought on, however; and, after he was killed in battle in 161 B.C., his brother Jonathan succeeded him. In 142 B.C., under the leadership of a third Maccabean brother, Simon, political independence from the Seleucids was finally achieved. Simon was also made hereditary high priest, giving the Maccabees (also called Hasmoneans) both political and religious control of the nation. Nothing like it had existed in Israel since the days of the Judges.

For just under eighty years the Hasmoneans were able to maintain the independence of the little nation, despite quarreling and intrigue between various rival members of the family. In 63 B.C., a fateful step was taken. One of the contending factions asked the Roman general, Pompey, to support its cause. The Romans came and took over. Jewish independence was lost, never again to be reconstituted until the establishment of modern Israel.

An Idumean soldier named Antipater worked hand-in-glove with the Romans; and his son, Herod, in 40 B.C. was named by them to rule Palestine. Herod was greatly disliked by the Jews, in part because he was an Idumean. Seeking to strengthen his position, he married a Hasmonean princess, the beautiful Mariamne. But he always feared her popularity, indeed was insanely suspicious and jealous of anyone who might be a rival, and executed several members of his own family, including Mariamne and three of his sons. Herod built the Temple in Jerusalem which Jesus knew, and was also the king reported by Matthew to have slain the babies of Bethlehem. He died in 4 B.C., perhaps a short time after Jesus' birth.

After Herod's death his kingdom was divided between three of his sons: Archelaus, ethnarch (governor of a province) of Judea, Idumea, and Samaria (4 B.C.–A.D. 6); Herod Antipas, tetrarch (governor of part of a province) of Galilee and Perea (4 B.C.–A.D. 39); and Herod Philip, tetrarch of the districts northeast of Galilee (4 B.C.–A.D. 34). Archelaus, unpopular with the Jews, was removed from office in A.D. 6 and banished to Gaul. From that date until A.D. 41 Judea, Samaria, and Idumea were under Roman procurators, among them Pontius Pilate (A.D. 26–36).

Palestinian Life in Jesus' Time

What was it like to live in Palestine in Jesus' day? To begin with, it was an occupied country. The Romans were there with a rough-handed justice which might occasionally inconvenience the average citizen, but for the most part provided stability. Of course, periodically there were uprisings among the Jews, especially among the hotheads who dreamed of independence through the coming of the expected Deliverer, the anointed of God. From time to time, Roman crosses raised along the roads with Jews hanging on them witnessed to the restlessness of the people.

Except for those living in cities such as Jerusalem or Capernaum, most Jews were farmers or herdsmen. They lived in flat-roofed, one-room clay houses in small villages and went out to the fields by day.

Much of the nation's wealth was concentrated in the hands of a few great landholders, the average person being a peasant laboring for a denarius a day. Fishing was a thriving industry in Galilee, the fish salted and exported to the world. The poles of life were worship and work, and the father who did not teach his son to be a worker was said by the rabbis to be teaching him to be a thief. Taxation was heavy, with a double burden of the demands of the often unscrupulous tax-farmers and publicans and the Jews' scrupulous conscience concerning the payment of tithes and other religious obligations. It is easy to understand the dislike the average Jew had for publicans and the contempt they held for fellow Jews who evaded their religious dues.

The everyday language was Aramaic, but Greek was the language of the world and was commonly spoken in Palestine. Despite efforts to preserve the separateness of Judaism, Greek influence was widespread. Roman roads, the Roman army, travel on the seas, the Greek language, and the exchange of products in trade had all contrived to open up the Mediterranean world. Jews were not isolated from such developments. Moreover, there had been a great dispersion of Jewish people throughout the ancient world. It is said that there were more Jews living in Alexandria, Egypt, in Jesus' day than lived in Jerusalem. These people maintained their loyalty to Judaism through the synagogue and, on occasion, through attendance at a festival in the Temple at Jerusalem. Such colonies of Jewish people were the objects of the first mission ventures of missionaries like Paul, who usually went first to the synagogue upon arrival in a city to preach the gospel.

Life in the time of Jesus was centered in the home, where children were regarded as a blessing from God. Parents considered it their sacred duty to instruct their children in the precepts of the Torah and to teach them reverence for their history as the people of God. The common experiences of family living—"when you sit in your house, and when you walk by the way, and when you lie down, and when you rise" (Deut. 6:7, RSV)—were media for transmitting the heritage of a chosen nation. In addition, there were special occasions when the great moments of Israel's history could be celebrated.

Religion in Jesus' Time

Only the necessity to organize one's description of life in Palestine in the time of Jesus warrants a separate section called "religion," for life was essentially impregnated with religious meaning. This has been observed in looking at the home. But certain particular features of this aspect of Jewish life need citing.

The central place occupied by the Scriptures, particularly the Law and the Prophets, deserves special note. Such is true also of the role of oral tradition, an accumulation of interpretations of the law which the Pharisees called "tradition of the elders," tracing the beginnings of the law to Moses. These oral interpretations were adaptations of the Torah and were designed to meet changing historical circumstances. Eventually this accumulated mass of application of the Torah was codified into the Mishnah, "second law," which in turn was amplified and explained to keep it relevant. The combined Mishnah and amplification (called Gemara) formed the Talmud. One of the sharpest points of contention between Jesus and the Pharisees was over the oral tradition, which Jesus contended had been elevated to a place properly belonging to the Scriptures.

While the Temple was the center of sacrificial worship of God and the symbol of his holy presence among his people, the synagogue served the common man by providing a place for assembly, for instruction in Torah, and for worship. There was one Temple; but synagogues, as neighborhood meetinghouses, were located everywhere there were Jews. A synagogue might be formed by ten families, and it is said that Jerusalem alone had more than four hundred synagogues in the time of Jesus. The synagogue was essentially a lay institution, presided over by a ruler chosen by his fellow members.

Religion was also maintained and promoted through such customs and practices as circumcision, dietary provisions, sabbath observance, sacrifice in the Temple, and special festivals. Two of the three major festivals were related to events in Israel's history. Passover, observed in the month of Nisan (March–April), recalled the deliverance from Egypt and God's saving action in the sacrifice of the Passover lamb. The Feast of Ingathering or Tabernacles (also called the Feast of Booths) was observed in the first month of the Jewish year, Tishri (September–October), and celebrated the gathering of the fruits of the year. It also was used to recall the wilderness wandering of Israel, and in celebration the people lived for seven days in booths. The third major festival was the Feast of Weeks or Firstfruits, also called Pentecost because it came fifty days after Passover, in the month of Sivan (May–June). This was a harvest festival used as a time of thanksgiving to God for his abundance. In addition, one fast day each year was to be observed as the Day of Atonement (*Yom Kippur*) on the tenth day of Tishri. This day was designed by elaborate ritual to celebrate the atonement of the nation's sins. Certain motifs characterize Israel's worship: recalling momentous events of God's mighty works on behalf of his people; recognition of sin and personal responsibility for it; contrition and confession; and joy and thanksgiving for the goodness of God.

The Chief Jewish Sects

Most Jews belonged to no special group, but certain groups represented points of view concerning the major religious issues. One such group was the Sadducees, the priestly party. They controlled the Temple, enjoyed high social standing as aristocrats of the Jews, and were tolerant and worldly in their outlook (especially toward Hellenism), and cooperative with the Roman occupation which kept them in power. Not all priests were Sadducees; some belonged to the Essenes. But the identification of priest and Sadducee was well-nigh universal. Being mainly concerned with the proper observance of the rituals of religion, they opposed the Pharisees on many grounds, particularly in the interpretation of the Scriptures. They were also bitter enemies of Jesus after he got to Jerusalem and began to threaten the establishment in the Temple.

The Pharisees, whose name seems to have come from a form of the word *parash*, "separated," probably developed out of the earlier Hasidim, "the Pious," of Maccabean days. They were never numerous, probably no more than six thousand, but were influential with the common people because of their dedication to religion. They believed the kingdom would come through keeping the law, and their concern was to further the knowledge and practice of it. The chief instruments to accomplish this were the synagogue and the oral tradition. The synagogue provided the setting and the oral tradition the lesson material for teaching the meaning of the law. In the long run, the Pharisees contributed most to the development of Judaism. Once the Temple was destroyed in A.D. 70 and the sacrificial system ended, it was the synagogue and the teaching that held Judaism together.

A brief reference to the scribes is warranted here. These "lawyers," career men in the study, copying, and interpretation of the law, also made a valuable contribution to the preservation of Judaism. Like the

Pharisees, they regarded Jesus with his appeal to the higher law of the spirit as a serious threat to the perpetuation and well-being of the faith of their fathers.

Being a scribe was a vocation, while being a Pharisee was belonging to a religious party. One might be both a scribe in work and a Pharisee in belief.

A third sect may also have derived from the Hasidim. These were Essenes who withdrew from public life to keep the stream of religion pure from contamination by the world. They lived a monastic, and frequently ascetic, existence—studying, copying, praying, and contemplating. While this group is not mentioned in the New Testament, it doubtless was a factor in the religious situation. It is even possible that John the Baptist, who prepared and preached in the wilderness east of Jerusalem where the Essenes lived, may have been familiar with their work.

A fourth group was the Zealots who, as their name suggests, were prepared to kill or be killed to resist Roman occupation. The origin of the Zealots is obscure, but there is a possibility that one of the twelve disciples had been a member. This was Simon, called Cananaean, a transliteration of the Aramaic word for Zealot.

Though it is an oversimplification of the views of these four sects, one can say that they represented four different ways of resisting Hellenism and the Roman occupation and of trying to insure the perpetuation of Judaism. The Pharisees sought to deal with the problem by increasing their own devotion to their religion and by encouraging other Jews to study it and live up to its precepts. The Sadducees wanted to preserve religion by promoting the practice of the cult, the rituals of sacrificial worship, and by cooperating with the Greco-Roman power structure. The Essenes undertook to save religion by withdrawing from the world and preserving a pure society. The Zealots thought the problem could best be solved with the instrument of a dagger (their name may have originated from the word *sicarius*, dagger).

Messianic Expectancy and the Forerunner

Jesus did not enter a world unprepared for his coming; "but when the time had fully come, God sent forth his Son" (Gal. 4:4, RSV). It was a time of unrest but also of expectancy. Centuries of hardship and persecution had driven Jews to a searching hunger for deliverance. During the heroic years of the Maccabean resistance, some of Israel's prophets expressed their confidence in intervention and deliverance by writing apocalyptic messages. These were "secret" documents containing hidden meanings which the uninformed could not understand but which were designed to encourage the faithful. This writing was like that in the book of Daniel, its purpose to urge Jews to stand firm in their faith since God's kingdom was at hand and the power of evil was about to be destroyed. With confident expectation, the faithful believed that deliverance would come through the appearance of an ideal ruler, a descendant of David, who would restore Israel's prestige and power among the nations and vindicate the faith of his people in the righteousness of God. This "day of the Lord" would witness the defeat of evil foes, a new covenant, and God's perfect righteous rule supplanting the imperfect rule of men.

John the Baptist was a witness to and a participant in this messianic hope. Luke 1:36 relates him by family to Jesus through their mothers, but the connection between John and Jesus is far more significant than blood kinship. This son of a priest filled a unique role in the coming of the Messiah. His training evidently included time spent in the region of the Essenes (Luke 1:80). His message was a stern call to repentance and to the performance of godly deeds based upon the announcement that "the kingdom of heaven is at hand" (Matt. 3:2), and that " 'after me comes he who is mightier than I, the thong of whose sandals I am not worthy to stoop down and untie' " (Mark 1:7, RSV). Thus, the Gospels all plainly say of John that his coming and his message were by divine direction, that he was unique in the plan of redemption as the forerunner of the Messiah, and that both he and the disciples plainly understood that he was not the Messiah nor in any sense his equal. The early church did not wish to shorten the shadow which John had cast. Indeed, had not the Lord himself said that "among those born of women none is greater than John" (Luke 7:28, RSV)? But it also did not want confusion to arise as to John's place in Messiah's work.

Not only in his preaching did John distinguish himself but also in his use of baptism as an act symbolizing repentance from sin and a new beginning. Crowds came out into the wilderness to hear this great prophet and to be immersed in the Jordan River. Baptism was not unique with John, of course, or with the Jews, who seem to have used it as proselyte initiation of Gentiles converting to Judaism. The Essenes used baptism for frequent ceremonial cleansing from sin. John evidently employed it as a sign of repentance. The early church saw baptism as having a more glorious symbolic significance—a participation by the believer in the death, burial, and resurrection of Christ (Rom. 6:3–4). John could not have given it that interpretation, of course, for he came before the resurrection. Perhaps this explains the reference in Acts 18:24–25 to Apollos as one who "knew only the baptism of John" (RSV), as well as the incident of Acts 19:1–7 about some disciples in Ephesus who had been baptized " 'into John's baptism' " (RSV). Nevertheless, John was a singular figure in the unfolding drama of redemption. He was the announcer of the coming of the King.

The Life of Jesus

What is known of the earthly life and ministry of Jesus comes almost entirely from the Gospels. Sermons of men like Peter, Stephen, and Paul, reported in the Acts, tell only a little of what Jesus did or said. Nor do the Letters or other writings of the New Testament fill the gaps. All of them are concerned with the world-changing impact of his death and resurrection and the nature of the new age and community that have come about as a result of these happenings.

Even so the Gospels cannot be properly regarded as biographies of Jesus. Two (Mark and John) tell nothing of his life until he began his ministry. Matthew and Luke report his miraculous birth; but, except for the one incident found in Luke 2:41–51, they are silent about his years in Nazareth until he was about thirty.

We can put down some firm pegs. For instance, Jesus was born no later than 4 B.C., the date of the death of Herod the Great, who was ruling in Judea at the time of Jesus' birth. John the Baptist began his ministry in the fifteenth year of the Emperor Tiberius, which would have been about A.D. 26. Presumably Jesus was baptized by John not long afterward and his ministry lasted probably no more than about two years. All of the Gospels fix the date of the crucifixion at a Passover, and only John mentions more than one Passover occurring during Jesus' ministry. He refers to three. These are some of the data which support the conclusion that the crucifixion and resurrection occurred around A.D. 29.

Jesus grew up in Nazareth, a small town fifteen miles west of the Sea of Galilee. By trade he was a carpenter (Mark 6:3). Joseph, his legal father, probably died before Jesus began his ministry, for he is never mentioned as being present. There were at least six other children in the family, including four brothers (Mark 6:3). His family was not sympathetic with what he was trying to do and say until after his resurrection. Then at least one of them, James, became a leader in the church at Jerusalem.

Jesus must have had the regular training of a Jewish boy in the synagogue. This would have included extensive study of the Scriptures, with which he was most familiar and which he liked to quote. But his work was really launched at his baptism, likely for him the act of consecration. The baptism was followed by the temptations in the wilderness. These are reported by Matthew and Luke, and may be understood as representative of unworthy and unacceptable approaches to the work he had dedicated himself to accomplish. Was he really God's Son? How would he reach his goals? How should he convince people of his sonship? By using his power to fill their stomachs with bread? By overwhelming them with the demonstration of supernatural power (jump from the pinnacle of the Temple)? Or by sweeping the nations of the world into his control (bow to Satan)? The temptations were real, but they did not occur only in the beginning of his ministry. They came to trouble him again and again as he went steadfastly to the cross.

The basic ministry of Jesus centered in Galilee. There he began to preach, teach, and heal. There he selected his inner circle of followers to be trained and then sent forth (Mark 3:14). He sent them forth not merely to give them "field practice," but to participate in the urgent task of announcing that the kingdom was at hand and that men should repent and believe. They were to preach and to heal and so show the power of the kingdom which had been released in their midst. Since they were to reach as many as possible, they were to travel light and move on when rejected.

Jesus' method of ministry was shocking and offensive to the religious establishment. He did not bypass the synagogues, but soon they were closed to him because of the nature of his message. Many Jews, either because they were too busy or too indifferent, did not keep the ceremonial regulations of Judaism. Such people were regarded as "sinners" by the pious, but Jesus received them and ate with them, which was terribly upsetting to groups like the Pharisees. Also, his friendship with tax collectors offended all who resented the Romans and the Jews who collaborated with them.

He not only associated with people who broke the ceremonial law, but was not slavish about observing it himself or requiring his disciples to do so. He clearly believed that the regulations established to insure the perpetuation of the tradition had become a hindrance to man's obedience of the higher law of God.

The Teaching of Jesus

Jesus announced the kingdom wherever he spoke, but it was more than a news bulletin. It was a command to become citizens of the kingdom of God by repentance and faith. A note of urgency and judgment was in his preaching, but the note of grace and love was there also. Jesus is perhaps as distinguished by the kind of people who responded to him as by those who found him offensive. "Good" people found it hard to accept a doctrine which called no man good but all men sinners needing to repent and receive forgiveness. But "sinners" heard the good news with joy. Our Lord taught and preached with freshness and authority. His approach was spontaneous and exciting. Using commonplace happenings, people, and objects as examples, he told parables of disarming simplicity to illustrate eternal truths.

By the kingdom of God Jesus did not mean something far removed from earth's realities. The kingdom is the reign of God over his people who have acknowledged that he is their Sovereign. God has entered the human arena and established his reign in the lives of people who will have it so. The kingdom is a present reality. It is here, but it is not here fully. God has firmly entrenched himself in our midst. He has established a beachhead and will not be driven into the sea. The time will come when the final victory will be achieved. It can already be anticipated, yet it is still in the future.

This message was also about God, who is not only the principal figure of history, but is Father. As Father he has acted personally to call persons to respond to his love with repentance and faith. Man's hope is not in his own goodness, for he is not ever good enough. Rather, it is in his repentance, a complete turning of the entire life, and an act of commitment to and trust in the willingness of God to forgive. This act of commitment is called faith, and it is more than giving assent to a proposition about God. It is the giving of one's life to a personal Lord. The life of commitment is nourished by worship, both public and private, and expressed in the acknowledgment of one's responsibility toward others. The life of faith as described in Jesus' teaching was never an abstraction or a theoretical proposition. It was always a call to act.

From Galilee to Jerusalem

At some point in his ministry, Jesus seems to have withdrawn from his public work to concentrate on the preparation of the twelve. In the area of Caesarea Philippi, located northeast of Galilee, a pivotal event took place in which Simon Peter, spokesman for the twelve, affirmed him as the Christ. Jesus asked that they not disclose his identity at that time (Mark 8:30), likely because he wished to have the next weeks or months with these men.

The event of Peter's confession marks a kind of watershed in Jesus' public ministry. His identity was further clarified by the experience of transfiguration. Soon thereafter he began to make his way toward Jerusalem. Luke wrote that "when the time was come that he should be received up, he stedfastly set his face to go to Jerusalem" (9:51). Matthew, Mark, and Luke devote large amounts of their material to this final journey and the events in Jerusalem which terminated in his crucifixion and resurrection. Along the way he told them openly of his approaching death. They all noted the urgency of his manner; and they were aware that Pharisees, scribes, Sadducees, the rich, the Zealots, and many others had a growing hostility toward him.

At length he came to Jerusalem in a noisy demonstration, riding upon the back of a donkey as an acted parable of his claim to be the Prince of peace. It has been called the Triumphal Entry, but it is more accurate to describe it as an open challenge. " 'The hour has come,' " he said (John 12:23, RSV). His entire incarnational mission had been by appointment. He had a rendezvous to keep. Driving the money changers from the Temple area, defying the priests by teaching in the Temple, telling parables which pointedly implied that God was going to take his "vineyard" from the ungrateful tenants and give it to those who would be faithful, and predicting the destruction of Jerusalem—all were acts of challenge. He was compelling them to decide for or against him. It was as if he said: "You have been talking about how to silence me. Well, here I am. Take me for what

I say I am, or else take me for what you say I am." He knew what the answer would be.

On the night of the Passover meal, Jesus sat with the twelve in a chamber borrowed for the evening that the group might observe the Passover together. He spoke tenderly to them but sadly revealed that there was a traitor in the midst. At some time in the course of the meal, Judas excused himself from the group and went to his appointment with the authorities to lead them to Jesus. In this upper room Jesus gave them a loaf and a cup, asking that each partake. As the Passover meal was the sacred occasion of remembering God's grace to his people in Egypt, this celebration of loaf and cup should be kept in grateful remembrance of his act of redemptive sacrifice.

John wrote that on this night he washed their feet to remind them of their obligation to serve one another in the ministry of forgiveness and cleansing. In words similar to the following, he spoke of his going away and of the coming and continued presence of the Holy Spirit: "Another Comforter just like me except that the world will not be able to lay hands on him as it is about to do to me because he will be among you and in you." The Comforter would continue Jesus' work and lead his people in their quest for understanding and fulfilment of God's purpose in Christ.

Then he went with them out of the crowded city to Mount Olivet which lay just across a little valley called Kidron, and there in a quiet garden took up a vigil of prayer.

It turned out to be a long night. Judas led the high priest's Temple police to the garden, identifying Jesus with a kiss of familiarity. The others fled. Peter, following at a distance, subsequently three times denied that he was one of them, and then wept with great remorse. When morning came, the governing body of the Jewish nation, called Sanhedrin, "The Seventy," assembled and made formal accusation of Jesus as a blasphemer deserving death. Inasmuch as the Romans did not permit the Jewish authorities the right of capital punishment, the prisoner, accused of being an insurrectionist, was sent to Pilate. The charge was thus changed from a religious to a political matter. Pilate was reluctant to accede, realizing that the prisoner deserved no such fate. But he appeased the Jewish leaders rather than create an ugly incident when Jerusalem was thronged by huge crowds of excited pilgrims come to celebrate the Feast of the Passover. It was a shabby bit of compromising; but Jesus was handed over to the soldiers for crucifixion, along with two bandits scheduled for execution who, unlike Barabbas, did not receive a pardon. Barabbas, a rebel and outlaw, had opportunity to learn that day what it was to have Jesus Christ literally die in one's place.

The crucifixion was carried out early on Friday morning. It was a terrible form of death, the crucified often lingering for days suspended from the beams by his hands and feet, slowly expiring from exhaustion and exposure. Death did not come from some mortal wound, but from gradual suffocation. As the body grew weaker, the victim was no longer able to push himself up sufficiently to get air into his lungs. The practice of breaking the prisoners' legs was not to determine if they were dead but to hasten the suffocation by incapacitating the legs. Jesus died after six hours on the cross, sooner than might have been anticipated. A well-to-do friend named Joseph of Arimathea arranged to have the body put in a new tomb nearby; but because it was nearing the end of Friday and the sabbath began at sundown, there was no time to perform the customary rites of anointing the body with spices. Wrapped in burial cloths, it was placed in the tomb and the huge cartwheel stone rolled in place to block the opening.

No event in history is more mysterious or better known than the resurrection. The evidence submitted in each of the four Gospels is that God raised Jesus up from death and that when women came to the tomb early on Sunday morning, the first day of the week, they found the tomb open and Jesus gone. The incredible news spread like wildfire. The disciples met him. He showed them his hands and feet. He was the same person they had known; yet he was not the same. There were occasions when those who had known him well before did not recognize him after his resurrection until he identified himself. He appeared and disappeared, unrestricted by the limitations of flesh. The fact of the resurrection is the basic and foundational reality of the gospel. Paul properly evaluated its indispensability to Christian faith when he wrote, "If Christ has not been raised, your faith is futile and you are still in your sins" (1 Cor. 15:17, RSV).

But the nature of the resurrection, like the nature of God himself, is beyond the capacity of our humanity to understand. Anybody who purports to "explain" the resurrection cannot be explaining the resurrection, for it is an act of God and we do not explain God. We experience him because he chooses to come to us and reveal himself to us in his mighty acts. The greatest of these is the resurrection of his Son, our Lord Jesus Christ. Paul can help us here by reminding us that the resurrection is no simple restoration of "flesh and blood" (1 Cor. 15:50). Like a sown seed springs up into a plant which is different from the seed but intimately related to the life that was locked up within it, so the physical life that is and the resurrected life that is to be are inseparably one.

The several accounts of the resurrection in the four Gospels are enriching. Like witnesses relating what they saw, each adds to our knowledge of this earthshaking event. To Luke we owe the record of the two men meeting him on the road to Emmaus and also his ascension from the Mount of Olives near Bethany, a suburb of Jerusalem. Luke and John tell of appearances to his disciples in their place of meeting in Jerusalem. Matthew tells of Jesus' appearance to them in Galilee, where on a mountain he charged them with the task of world mission. John's Gospel contains the moving encounter of the doubting Thomas with the risen Lord and of the restoration of Peter beside the Lake of Galilee one early dawn. All report the initial discovery of the resurrection by the women. John names only Mary Magdalene, adding also the confirmation of the examination of the empty tomb by two of the disciples, Peter and another (presumably John himself).

Such is the physical evidence of the event which Christians see as the most decisive moment in history. Transformed lives of multitudes who experienced and continue to experience the presence of the risen Lord confirm the Gospel event. In wonder, the church beheld the cross and the empty tomb. It did not look upon the two events as contradictory, but as one mighty act of God of which it could only say in ceaseless praise, "Behold, what manner of love the Father hath bestowed upon us" (1 John 3:1).

CHAPTER SEVEN

Places and People
of the
New Testament
Part II—The Community
of Faith

The story of Jesus Christ does not end with his death. Had he been only a teacher, prophet, or just a good man, our interest in him would be limited to historical inquiry. But his resurrection was like an explosion that set off a chain reaction of global proportions. It gave permanence to the community of faith, the church, and "the powers of death shall not prevail against it" (Matt. 16:18, RSV). It vindicated his teachings and the claim he made for himself. It fired his followers with unquenchable hope and confidence in God's ultimate triumph over evil. It provided the basis for understanding not only what had happened but what the future held in store.

Moreover, the risen Christ continued to be experienced among and in them through the Holy Spirit. That was the significance of Pentecost. The disciples understood the event as validation of his promise to be with them forever. Luke, author of Acts, makes this plain in his opening words: "In the first book [Gospel of Luke], . . . I have dealt with all that Jesus began to do and teach, until the day when he was taken up" (Acts 1:1–2, RSV). "Began" implies that Acts will continue the story already partly told.

The Church in Jerusalem

On the day of Pentecost, fifty days after Jesus' crucifixion, God affirmed his work among the followers of Jesus through the coming of the Holy Spirit. During those exciting days since the resurrection, they had been following instructions "not to depart from Jerusalem" (Acts 1:4, RSV), and they had used the time well. One of them, Matthias, was chosen as an apostle to replace the traitor, Judas; and in the process they delineated the requirements for apostleship. One must be a witness to the resurrection and also have been a participant in the work of Jesus from the ministry of John the Baptist to the resurrection of Jesus. Certainly an apostle must have been appointed by the Lord (Acts 1:25). Needless to say, few could qualify on the first two points; and later the regulations likely were relaxed, else it is doubtful that such outstanding church leaders as Barnabas and Paul could have been apostles.

The coming of the Holy Spirit at Pentecost was crucial in the church's life. The Spirit came not just upon the apostles but upon all, and all began to witness. Luke makes it plain that a miracle occurred, that God's mighty power moved three thousand to repent, believe, and be baptized. Peter's sermon, used by Luke as illustrative of apostolic preaching, interpreted the amazing happening of Pentecost as the fulfilment of the Old Testament prophet Joel. He recounted the glorious events of Jesus Christ and called for decision. Thus began the church's outreach in Jerusalem.

There was another aspect of the ministry of the early church: the development of a community marked by prayer, teaching, and fellowship. The large numbers of people who had embraced the faith in Christ and who wished to remain in the community at Jerusalem constituted a problem. They had to be fed. A voluntary system of sharing was developed to take care of the poor. Sometimes the arrangement worked. Unselfish and godly people like Barnabas, a native of Cyprus, sold their property and gave the proceeds to the church. On other occasions it did not work, as in the case of Ananias and Sapphira whose deceit threatened the mutual trust and well-being of the community.

Ugly accusations of discrimination against those who had come to Jerusalem from outside Palestine began to be heard. These were the "Hellenists," as distinguished from the "Hebrews," native-born Palestinians. Both groups were Jewish. The result of this controversy was the church's selection of seven men to see to the distribution of food. All of the seven had Greek names and may therefore have belonged to the Hellenists. It is instructive to remember that this group, rather than the twelve, furnished the leadership for the mission thrust beyond the confines of Judaism. One of the seven, Stephen, was martyred for his insistence that the Jewish nation did not have a monopoly on God's grace. Another, Philip, preached to the Samaritans and also baptized an Ethiopian "God-fearer," that is, a non-Jew drawn to the high principles of Jewish monotheism.

The way was being prepared for the breakthrough of the gospel to the Gentile world. The theme of the Acts has been said to be "unhindered." [1] The Holy Spirit was leading the church to take down the barriers that hindered the free course of the gospel wherever men would hear, repent, and believe.

Jewish Christian and Non-Christian

In the early days of the church, the Sadducees, priests, and Temple police were extremely annoyed by the preaching of the apostles. Their opposition was chiefly that the preachers were a nuisance. They kept coming to the Temple and cluttering up the area, disrupting the even flow of Temple business. On at least two occasions (Acts 4:3; 5:17–18), apostles were arrested at the instigation of the Sadducean party. And in one of the first reported discussions of the new movement by the Sanhedrin (seventy members about evenly divided between Sadducees and Pharisees), it was a well-known Pharisee, Gamaliel, who came to the defense of the Christians. (This was likely the same man who taught Paul.)

The attitude of the Sadducees may indicate that the opposition to the new movement was at first more practical than theological in nature. But the ground of opposition shifted as the implications of faith in Christ became clear, and particularly after men like Stephen began to be heard to say that God had not bound himself to the Jewish people or to the Temple but that his purpose was to call his people from the ends of the earth. Thus the movement came to be more than a nuisance. It was regarded as sheer heresy; and those guardians of the faith, the Pharisees, became involved and resolved to stamp it out. Stephen was martyred; James was put to the sword by Herod Agrippa I; Peter was arrested; and the spokesmen of a worldwide gospel driven from Jerusalem.

It is interesting that the twelve apostles were able to remain in Jerusalem after the outburst of hostility that took Stephen's life. Was their preaching of the universal call of Christ less "inflammatory" than others'? The church continued in Jerusalem for several decades after Stephen's death, its relations with Judaism being reasonably cordial. Some in the Jerusalem church were strict observers of Jewish regulations and were very upset, for example, because Peter went to the house of Cornelius and ate with Gentiles (Acts 11:3). As late as the time of the conference at Jerusalem over the relationship between the Jewish and Gentile elements in the movement, there were Pharisees in the Jerusalem church (Acts 15:5).

But the Holy Spirit's leadership of the church to "go into all the world and make disciples" brought inevitable alienation between Jewish Christians and non-Christian Jews. For many years James, the brother of Jesus, was leader of the church in Jerusalem and was held in high regard by non-Christian Jews. However, relationships steadily deteriorated and in A.D. 62, James was assassinated by an anti-Christian group.

The Jews were not always able to remain free of oppression, either. Toward the end of Nero's reign, the Jews of Palestine revolted. The Roman procurators found their fiercely independent spirit difficult to understand, and they could not keep order. In A.D. 66, open revolt erupted, signaled by cessation of the regular sacrifices offered in the Temple on behalf of the emperor, a practice which had served as a substitute for emperor worship. The revolt was finally quelled by the Romans in A.D. 70 with appalling bloodshed and the destruction of the Temple. Once again in A.D. 130, the Jews revolted against Rome in protest of the Emperor Hadrian's decision to rebuild and rename Jerusalem, constructing a temple to Jupiter on the site of the Temple of God. Led by a certain Bar Cochba, who was hailed by some of the Jews as the Messiah, the rebels fought with ferocity but were no match for Roman power. In A.D. 135, the revolt was crushed and all Jews were expelled from the city.

Early in the rebellion, Christians of Jerusalem fled the city and went to Pella, a Gentile city a few miles east of the Sea of Galilee. Some of them returned after the revolt was put down. Jews did not forget that the Christians had left Jerusalem in the crisis. A man named Symeon, said to be a cousin of Jesus, was leader of the church in Jerusalem after the revolt of A.D. 66–70, but he was martyred in A.D. 104. Jewish Christians who continued loyal to Jewish legal practices were known as Ebionites, a Hebrew word meaning "poor"; but they had a dwindling significance in the life of the church.

By the end of the first century of the Christian era, relationships between Christian and non-Christian Jews had been strained to the breaking point. For example, one of the prayers of benediction used in the synagogue service was so revised as to make it impossible for a Christian to pray it. Since the Eighteen Benedictions were a required part of synagogue worship, Christian Jews could no longer participate. If one asks what happened to the Jewish Christians, one can only speculate that they either drifted off to the fringes as the Ebionites, or else eventually gave up their distinctive Jewishness and became identified with Gentile Christianity.

The Church in the Roman World

The gospel spread from Jerusalem mainly into the Roman world. It may have gone east of Palestine into Arabia and Mesopotamia and farther east into Parthia. It may have gone southeast into the Nabatean Arab empire; but if it did, we have little evidence of it. The arena of Christian mission in the New Testament age was largely the Roman Empire. At first the church was relatively safe from oppression by the Romans, in part because of the government's policy of religious toleration and in part because the earliest Christians were nearly all Jewish and shared the protection enjoyed by Judaism as one of the recognized or "licit" religions of the Empire. As the rift between Jews and Christians became wider, this shelter was lost to the church. An example of hostility between Jew and Christian may be reflected in a report by the Roman historian, Suetonius, who wrote that during the reign of the Emperor Claudius (A.D. 41–54), he expelled the Jews from Rome because they were rioting at the instigation of a certain Chrestus. This may be a confused report of the fact that there was trouble between the Jews in Rome because some were Christians and others were opposed to Christianity.

In the reign of Nero, who was looking for a scapegoat to blame for the great fire in A.D. 64, Christians suffered fierce persecution at Roman hands. That case appears to have been confined to Rome, however, and there was no general persecution throughout the empire until the reign of Domitian (A.D. 81–96), who sought to enforce the long-existing requirement that all Roman subjects worship the emperor as a deity. Many Christians, unable to accede to this demand and remain true to their faith, were martyred as "atheists," including some occupying high places in the government. Intermittent periods of persecution of Christians occurred in the Roman Empire until the end of the third century A.D.

The Roman world did not lack for religions. In addition to emperor worship, which was an expression of patriotism for the most part, there was a nearly inexhaustible supply of religions built upon myths and legends concerning the gods of Egypt, Greece, and Rome. One might be a devotee of Isis and Osiris of Egypt, of Dionysus, the Greek god of wine, and Demeter, goddess of grain, and a half dozen others at the same time. One need not be exclusive unless one belonged to the monotheistic Judeo-Christian tradition. The mystery religions, promising adherents the secrets of life through initiation into the cult, were also very popular. Luke's comment about the Athenians may not have been literally true of all first-century people, but it is descriptive of the general condition: "Now all the Athenians and the foreigners who lived there spent their time in nothing except telling or hearing something new" (Acts 17:21, RSV).

Paul, Least and Greatest

No accounting for the advance of the gospel across the Roman world is possible except for the apostle Paul. Born in Tarsus of Cilicia, "no mean city," he was ideally suited to the work for which God had singled him out. A Roman citizen, a Jew of the strictest sect of Pharisees, a man of Greek learning and also schooled in Jerusalem at the feet of one of its most celebrated rabbis (Gamaliel), he had all the credentials to be what he later said he was, "a chosen vessel."

Consider the experiences of Paul: his conversion near Damascus; his blindness and subsequent restoration of sight and acceptance by the Christians whom he had come to arrest; his preaching of Jesus as the Son of God in the synagogues of the very city to which he had brought bills of indictment against Jews who followed "the Way"; his flight from Damascus and his stay in Arabia; his brief return to Jerusalem after an absence of three years; his indebtedness to Barnabas who trusted him and vouched for him when others in the Jerusalem church were suspicious and skeptical that he could have made such a complete turnabout; and his return to his home city of

Tarsus. All of these are part of the familiar story of this extraordinary man's preparation for the great mission thrust which was to come through his efforts. Acts 9; 22; 26; Galatians 2, and 2 Corinthians 11 all relate these events.

When the church at Antioch began to receive into membership large numbers of Gentiles and not simply isolated individuals (as in the case of Peter's preaching to Cornelius at Caesarea), the church at Jerusalem sent the ever-faithful Barnabas to look into the situation. He came and saw a whole new world opening and immediately thought of Saul as the man best prepared to preach the gospel to the Gentiles, so he went to Tarsus and brought Saul to Antioch.

There followed an exciting year of ministry in Antioch. This great missionary church, which now became the base of mission operations into the Roman world, was led by the Holy Spirit to send Barnabas and Saul on a preaching tour into Asia Minor. While on this tour, Saul emerged as the leader and began to be referred to as Paul, his Roman name. Also on this tour the ground was laid for the subsequent disagreement between these two godly men, Paul and Barnabas. John Mark, a kinsman of Barnabas, had become disenchanted for some unknown reason and left the tour after it had begun. Paul refused to take John Mark on the next mission, creating such a rift that Paul and Barnabas went their separate ways. Barnabas took Mark and went to his native Cyprus, while Paul took Silas and went overland to Galatia, and later to Macedonia and Greece.

Law and Grace

It was now evident that Gentiles were embracing the gospel in large numbers, and the conservative Jewish Christians were extremely upset that these people were coming into the stream of the Judeo-Christian faith without accepting the requirements of the law regarding such matters as circumcision and the dietary regulations. To the Jewish Christians, it appeared that Gentile Christians were bypassing the great heritage of God's people. Moreover, it seemed to be a clear case of setting the Scriptures aside, for did not the Scriptures teach these things? Some of the more zealous of the brethren from Jerusalem took it upon themselves to correct Paul's faulty evangelism. They began to follow him wherever he went, telling Gentile converts that they had not received the whole gospel when they believed the doctrine of justification by faith. This infuriated

Paul, who felt that these "Judaizers" were perverting the gospel, making it into a new form of legalism. Nothing in all of Paul's life affected him more deeply. He was a man of strong conviction, and the seriousness with which he took this dispute over law and grace is clearly reflected in his letter to the Galatians. There he made an impassioned plea that they not desert the gospel of grace for the empty bag of salvation by works.

The matter finally came to a head in Jerusalem where a conference of church leaders was convened. Acts 15 gives an account of this meeting; it is one of the most significant chapters of the Bible. God's miraculous acts of grace among the Gentiles were recited by Peter, who took the role of mediator between the extremes. Then Paul and Barnabas were heard, after which James, the Lord's brother and a representative of the more conservative elements of the church, spoke. He acknowledged the validity of the Gentile mission, but he also felt deeply for his Jewish brethren of the Dispersion who would be offended by a gospel which seemed to ignore the law of Moses. Therefore, he suggested that concerning Jewish laws Gentile Christians be asked to observe a limited number of obligations. These were commonly known as the "precepts of Noah," and were recommended for Gentiles who wished to establish good relationships with Jews. These precepts included abstaining from immorality, worship of idols, eating meat strangled, or consumption of blood. That was the agreement reached by the convocation in Jerusalem. Paul must have been gratified at the decision, for it meant a victory for justification by faith alone. The "precepts of Noah" would in any event be observed by a conscientious Christian.

Paul was by no means an enemy of the law of Moses. He reverenced it, calling it a "tutor" leading man to Christ. But he saw the law's bankruptcy as a means of redemption. Indeed, he said that the law only increased his despair without God's grace because he took it seriously enough to realize that it sharpened his sense of sin. Still, God's grace was no license to sin. "Are we to continue in sin that grace may abound?" he once wrote, and answered the rhetorical question emphatically: "By no means! How can we who died to sin still live in it?" (Rom. 6:1–2, RSV). Nonetheless, he was certain that redemption is possible only by God's grace expressed in the death and resurrection of his Son, Jesus Christ, and appropriated by an act of total commitment, which Paul believed to be the meaning of faith. By such faith in God's redemptive love, Abraham had been saved; by such faith we are saved.

The law-grace controversy did not end with the conference in Jerusalem, but continued to hound Paul and hinder his efforts. He made a third mission tour, this time remaining three years in the strategic city of Ephesus, chief center of the Roman province of Asia (modern-day Turkey). From time to time he wrote letters to the churches which he had helped to establish. Around the year A.D. 58, he went back to Jerusalem, carrying a large love offering painstakingly collected from among the Gentile Christians as an expression of brotherly love toward Jewish Christians in want. There, he was falsely accused of bringing a Gentile into the court of Israel and thereby violating the Temple. He was set upon by a mob intent on lynching him.

Paul's Last Years

Rescued by the Romans, Paul was subsequently sent to Caesarea, Roman capital of the province of Syria, when it was learned that he was a Roman citizen and not some riffraff or outlaw. There he languished in jail for two years, waiting for his case to come to trial. The governor was a rapacious and corrupt man named Felix, who, having heard Paul preach of "justice and self-control and future judgment" (Acts 24:25, RSV), put him off about deciding his case, hoping that Paul would arrange to give him a bribe. When the next governor, Festus, arrived, he sought to have Paul's case settled and was about to decide to send him back to Jerusalem for trial. Paul, however, fearful that a return to Jerusalem would end in his assassination, exercised his prerogative as a Roman citizen to have his case reviewed by Caesar. Thus did Paul finally get to Rome, a city he had long wanted to visit in order to preach there before going westward to Spain.

Paul's voyage to Rome as a prisoner of the government and the shipwreck in a storm on the Mediterranean Sea is graphically told in Acts 27. After a three-month stay on the island of Malta following the shipwreck, he was put on board a vessel bound for Italy. At last he came to Rome. After two years in Rome, during which time he enjoyed relative freedom under "house arrest," living in his own quarters and receiving all who came to see him, Paul's story abruptly ends in Acts. From a reading of some of the letters of the New Testament, and from the traditions about him, many conclude that Paul was released after the two-year stay in Rome and went on his way, perhaps to Spain and later back to Asia Minor, there to be arrested again, brought to Rome, and executed. No one knows why Luke left Paul's case "up in the air." Did he plan a sequel? Is the ending of Acts missing? Or did Luke do exactly what he intended to do—show how the gospel emerged "openly and unhindered" (Acts 28:31, RSV) in the Roman world?

The contribution of Paul is incalculable. Despite the handicap of a physical ailment, a "thorn in the flesh" (2 Cor. 12:7), that at least once caused him to despair of his life and probably nagged him continually, he exhibited an amazing hardiness, traveling all over the Roman world with relentless courage and determination to preach the gospel. He was a strong man with deep convictions, a man capable of great appreciation and compassion. His work as "apostle to the Gentiles" laid the foundation of western Christendom. By the end of the first century, Jewish Christians were a tiny minority in the church and were moving farther and farther away from the mainstream of Christian mission. Paul was the instrument which the Holy Spirit had employed to break down the walls and make of the gospel a universal faith. But perhaps his greatest contribution was in his letters in the New Testament. Here we see the real man, and we see the conditions existing in the early churches and the gospel interpreted for this and every age.

Tradition has it that Paul was beheaded during the Neronian persecution, about A.D. 64. The church was beginning to lose its first-line leaders. James, Jesus' brother, had been lynched in Jerusalem in A.D. 62, and the tradition holds that Peter was crucified head downward in Rome about the same time Paul was beheaded. What would happen to the church now that those "who had been with him from the beginning" were disappearing? This question provided the basis for the development of a body of literature of the Christian faith which would hold the church together, help it to understand the gospel and the nature of its mission, and prevent the faith from being gradually altered by the pressure of circumstance. That is why we have the New Testament.

The Obscure Decades[2]

The next thirty-five or forty years are critically important to the life of the church, but we know little about the period. It is as if the church had entered a tunnel; and when it came out, certain new trends were seen emerging. At the entrance of the tunnel, we are at the end of the first generation of Christendom. Leaders like Peter, James, and Paul were passing away, but who their successors were is almost unknown. Who were the "second generation" churchmen? Men like Timothy and Titus were introduced as Paul's "sons in the ministry," but not too much is known of their work.

Other than Paul's letters, most of the New Testament was written during these obscure decades. Except for 2 Peter and possibly the Gospel of John, the New Testament had all been written by the beginning of the second century A.D. The dating of John's Gospel is still questioned. It reflects conditions in the world and in the church which are somewhat later than those known in the other three Gospels. But it cannot be much later than the end of the first century A.D., because a papyrus fragment of this Gospel dating about A.D. 130 was discovered in Egypt a few years ago. It is positive, therefore, that the Gospel of John was known in Egypt by the third decade of the second century.

During the thirty-five years between the death of Peter and Paul and the beginning of the second century, strong churches had been established all over the Roman world. Churches existed, gospel materials were being copied and rewritten, and an extensive Christian literature was being developed in Egypt during the first half of the second century. The churches in Asia Minor were quite strong, too, particularly those around Ephesus. The book of Revelation, usually believed to have been written during the persecution of Christians by the Emperor Domitian in the last decade of the first century, tells of the progress of the gospel in this area.

In Syria the stronghold of Christianity was the church at Antioch. It had been the great mission church that gave the impetus to world missions by commissioning and sending out Paul, Barnabas, Silas, and others. At the beginning of the second century A.D., this remarkable church had accepted a church order that called for rule by a monarchical bishop. In the year A.D. 107, the bishop of Antioch, Ignatius, was seized and taken to Rome for martyrdom in the arena. As he traveled to Rome, he was met along the way by other bishops of churches. He also wrote a series of letters in which he called upon the churches to accept the rule of the bishops and to resist the encroachments of Judaistic legalism and Gnostic doctrines in the churches. These letters reflect that some of the conditions seen in the Gospel of John and the Johannine letters still troubled the churches. They also reflect a trend in church organization. Ignatius' strong plea on behalf of the bishops suggests that many churches were not willing to accept the rule of the bishop, but others had already done so.

Churches existed also in Bithynia and Pontus, in Macedonia, Athens, Corinth, Crete, and, of course, Rome. Indeed, in nearly every population center of the empire a "colony of the kingdom" was established by the beginning of the second century A.D.

The Emerging Church

As the New Testament era closed, certain trends were emerging. One was reliance upon a body of literature as inspired Scripture. A great deal of material had been produced about Jesus Christ and his movement. What should be considered essential? Near the middle of the second century, a crisis arose which compelled the making of some decisions about this matter. A church leader from Pontus named Marcion was imbued with Gnostic doctrines that denied Jesus' humanity and renounced the Old Testament. Marcion sought to eliminate from Christian Scriptures all of the Old Testament, plus all of the New Testament except Luke and certain of the Pauline letters. Marcion's influence was considerable, causing serious schism in the church before he was declared to be a heretic. The effect was to make the church think more seriously about the importance of the Scriptures.

Toward the end of the first century, the church had begun to reappraise its hope for an early end of the world. The apostolic church had been excited over the prospect of an early conclusion of history and the second coming of Christ. This matter dominates the thought of 1 and 2 Thessalonians, for example. But as time passed and the Lord did not return, a reevaluation of this expectancy became necessary. It was seen that many of the promises which had been identified with the second coming of Christ had already been fulfilled in his resurrection and the coming of the Holy Spirit. The believers were actually living in the new age already; and, although they never surrendered confidence in a final "eschaton" and the end of the world, they now saw that God's timetable was not available to them and that "with the Lord one day is as a thousand years, and a thousand years as one day" (2 Peter 3:8, RSV).

There are no creeds in the church which emerged from the New Testament era, but there are certain simple confessions of faith. These confessions are always Christ-centered, and they always employ Old Testament terms to express who Jesus is and what is his role. Some are very brief: " 'Jesus is Lord' " (1 Cor. 12:3, RSV); "Jesus Christ is Lord" (Phil. 2:11); "Lord and Christ" (Acts 2:36); "Christ, the Son of the living God" (Matt. 16:16); " 'the Lamb of God, who takes away the sin of the world' " (John 1:29, RSV); and others. Some confessions, such as Philippians 2:5–11, were more inclusive in their scope and described not only Christ's identity but his mission.

These confessions of faith were used in public worship, as also were psalms from the Old Testament or Christian hymns written to be sung in praise of God. Worship was usually on the first day of the week to celebrate the Lord's resurrection, and might include also a gospel appeal, called *kerygma,* "proclamation," and a period of moral instruction, *didache,* "teaching." Those making confession of Jesus Christ as Lord were baptized by immersion.

Early in church history the Lord's Supper had been connected with a church supper, or fellowship meal. Evidently the fellowship meal led to dissension and excess in some instances, for example, at Corinth (1 Cor. 11:17–32), and was later discontinued or at least separated from the observance of the Lord's Supper.

Strong organization has played a prominent role in the life of the church through the centuries, but the development of church hierarchies was later than the New Testament period. The close of the New Testament era witnesses no hierarchy and the translation of the New Testament Greek word *episkopos* as bishop in the authoritarian sense is misleading. *Episkopos* was a formal title and did not designate an office. Rather, it described the work or function of an "elder." The elders were charged with the work of "overseeing," which is the meaning of "bishop." The New Testament has no office with the title of "bishop," granting a rank superior to that of the elders of the church.

One final word should be said about the church's emergence into the second century. It was careful to exalt Jesus Christ as Lord and Head of the church. Its foundation was set in the soil of Palestine where God had come in the human and historical life of Jesus of Nazareth, now seen to be the risen and eternal Lord, the Head of the church.

---

[1] Frank Stagg, *The Book of Acts* (Nashville: Broadman Press, 1955).

[2] A designation used by Floyd V. Filson, *A New Testament History* (Philadelphia: Westminster Press, 1964), p. 295.

CHAPTER EIGHT

How the
New Testament
Came to Be

There is reason for the arrangement of the New Testament. Matthew's Gospel, emphasizing Jesus as the fulfilment of the promises concerning the coming of the Messiah, forms a kind of bridge between the Old Covenant and the New. The Revelation, with its apocalyptic vision of the end of history, is an appropriate conclusion. But the books were not written in the order in which they appear in the Bible. If you were to rearrange them chronologically, the list would appear strikingly different. Matthew would be far from the first, and Revelation would not be the last. All of Paul's letters would probably come before any of the Gospels, and they might be listed as follows: 1 and 2 Thessalonians, Galatians, 1 and 2 Corinthians, Romans, Philippians, Philemon, Colossians, and Ephesians.*
The Pastoral Epistles must be placed last, although the time and circumstance of their writing is a matter of debate.

If you continued the chronological arrangement of New Testa-

---

*Editor's Note: As in the case of Old Testament dates and authors of books, these New Testament dates are the studied opinion of the writer of this volume and are not undisputed by other scholars. Space in this book does not allow for a full discussion of these matters. This material will be dealt with more fully, and varied opinions presented, in the three New Testament survey books.

ment writings, after Paul's letters the remainder might read something like this: Mark, Matthew, Luke-Acts, 1 Peter, 1 and 2 Timothy, Titus, Hebrews, James, Revelation, Gospel of John, 1, 2, and 3 John, Jude, and 2 Peter. The history of the early church and its development by response to the challenge of the secular world becomes clearer when the New Testament books are considered in chronological sequence.

How the Gospels Came to Be Written

Because there would be no gospel without Jesus Christ, we easily assume that the four Gospels, the major source of knowledge of his life, should be studied first. It is instructive, however, to recall that for the first generation after the beginning of the church there were no documents called Gospels, indeed, no Scripture except the Old Testament. The gospel made its way through the Roman Empire without recorded Gospels. As has been said, "Life always precedes literature, and we do well to remember that the Good News was being proclaimed before any Christian literature existed at all." [1]

From the study of the only primary historical account we have of the apostolic church, Luke's Acts, it will be seen that the media of the spread of the gospel were preaching and the life of the church. Men like Peter, Stephen, Philip, and Paul went forth announcing that certain things had happened which proved that Jesus of Nazareth was the long-awaited Messiah, and that the time had come for all to repent and believe. The specific things emphasized were his death on the cross and his resurrection. No doubt apostolic preaching filled in the details of his life. But the important fact to remember is that they were more concerned to stress Jesus' death and resurrection than to recite his teachings or to report his many acts of loving-kindness toward those in need. It is not without significance that Paul is reported in the Acts as attracting the attention of the Athenians "because he preached Jesus and the resurrection" (Acts 17:18, RSV), or that he himself wrote to the Corinthians, "For I decided to know nothing among you except Jesus Christ and him crucified" (1 Cor. 2:2, RSV).

The other medium of evangelism in the Roman world was the church. Bands of believers, often meeting in houses or on hillsides and frequently in hiding, offered to the unbelieving world an impressive body of evidence that Christ is Lord. So, before the Gospels were written, there were both preaching and the church. Out of these came the written records, inspired by the Holy Spirit.

Is this to suggest, then, that early Christians had no interest in the life and teachings of Jesus? Would this mean that their only concern was to announce the *kerygma,* the saving news of his death and resurrection, and to establish churches, communities of redemption, where others could be drawn to hear the saving word? Not at all. These "evangelistic sermons" were preached to the unbelieving world and the church was witnessing by its life to the validity of the claims concerning Christ at the same time those who had known him in the flesh were passing on the information which was later to make up a large part of the written Gospels. Thus, those who had come to him as their risen Lord without having known him in the flesh learned the gospel.

What Jesus had said and done was treasured by the church. Never had anyone spoken or acted as he. It would be unthinkable that the church should treat lightly or handle carelessly the priceless gift of his human life. But at first the evidence of Jesus was preserved and transmitted orally in the form of lessons or sermons. These were not organized into chronological accounts or made into a continuous and connected "biography." Instead, it appears more likely that the material came together first as "units" of individual incidents, parables, and sayings; and these were used in the life of the church when it worshiped or examined the moral issues of its day or sought to answer its critics. That was the period of the eyewitness, a time of which it has been said, "Christian hands are full of jewels, but there is no desire to weave a crown." [2]

However, the time came "to weave a crown," to write permanent records of this unique Life which had split history in two. It became evident that the first-generation Christians were passing away. Soon no one would be left who could say, "I was with him in the flesh." Behind the four Gospels were many accounts of Jesus, both oral and written, which in no way detract from the Gospels' validity and authority. Luke himself in his introductory sentence declared that he approached his task with the purpose of setting down "an orderly account." Luke wrote: "Inasmuch as many have undertaken to compile a narrative of the things which have been accomplished among us, just as they were delivered to us by those who from the beginning were eyewitnesses and ministers of the word" (Luke 1:1–2,

RSV). Luke, a second-generation believer, recognized the need for such a work because eyewitnesses were disappearing. Also, he was not a pioneer in recording the work of Jesus; many had undertaken it before him. Out of this felt need for a historical record which could be the touchstone of Christian faith for all time to come the Gospels were written.

The Synoptic Gospels

Even a casual reading of the four Gospels will reveal something that has long impressed people who study the New Testament— Matthew, Mark, and Luke are strikingly similar while John is strikingly different. So alike are the first three that they are commonly known as the Synoptic Gospels, since they look together at the same subject and present a common view. Various explanations have been offered for this similarity, including the hypothesis that all three had a common oral Aramaic source. That explanation might seem plausible except for two facts: (1) there are too many cases in the Synoptics where identical language, not merely a similarity or paraphrase, appears in all three (compare Matt. 9:6; Mark 2:10; Luke 5:24); (2) there are too many differences between what the individual Gospels include or omit to support the argument for a common oral Aramaic source.

The thesis receiving widest support concerning the origin of the Synoptics is that both Matthew and Luke had access to Mark's Gospel, plus another source of material not in Mark, and in addition Matthew and Luke each included some Gospel material not found anywhere else. The evidence certainly points to Mark as the earliest Gospel. Matthew used nearly all of Mark (606 verses out of 661 in Mark), and Luke nearly half. Matthew and Luke frequently repeat Mark's exact words. More than half of Mark's language reappears in both Matthew and Luke. Matthew and Luke commonly follow Mark's order of events, and when one of them disagrees with Mark's order the other agrees with Mark.

Although some scholars date Mark as early as A.D. 50, it appears probable that the earliest Gospel was written in Rome about the year A.D. 65 by John Mark, youthful resident of Jerusalem in Jesus' time, kinsman of Barnabas, and companion of Paul. An ancient tradition says that he was closer to Peter than to Paul, and that his Gospel is largely the record of Peter's personal recollections. Be that as it may, this is the briefest, most descriptive, and succinct of the Gospels. It omits any reference to Jesus' birth but opens with the beginning of his ministry, and closes with the simple, straightforward report of the morning of his resurrection.

In looking at Matthew and Luke, one discovers that they share with each other some material not found in Mark. There are over two hundred such verses, including many sayings of Jesus, particularly in the Sermon on the Mount. This material, whose source is unidentifiable, is often called "Q" (for the German word *quelle,* meaning source). "Q" may have been one of the "many [who] have undertaken to compile a narrative" (RSV), about whom Luke wrote in his opening sentence. It could have been a collection of Jesus' sayings or a manual of moral instruction for new believers. Whatever it was, it is a fact that both Matthew and Luke have drawn from some common source which they often used nearly verbatim.

If we look further into Matthew and Luke, we discover that each has material unique in his own Gospel. Matthew has more than three hundred verses found nowhere else, including the account of the Wise Men and Herod at Jesus' birth, Judas' suicide, Pilate's handwashing, and much of the Sermon on the Mount. Luke has more than four hundred verses which appear in no other Gospel, including much of the material between Luke 9:51 and 18:14, the section containing such priceless gems as the parables of the good Samaritan, the prodigal son, and the Pharisee and publican. Matthew's Gospel must have appeared after Mark's, possibly in the 80's, and is believed to have been written somewhere in Palestine by a Jewish Christian teacher (Matthew) who was eager to establish the connection between Old Testament prophecies concerning the Messiah and Jesus of Nazareth in whom they have been fulfilled. He organized his material topically, as if wanting to provide a Gospel useful in the instruction of converts. Five main "discourses" bring together sayings of Jesus: the Sermon on the Mount (chaps. 5–7); the charge to the twelve (chap. 10); parables of the kingdom (chap. 13); instruction for community life (chap. 18); and the end of the age (chaps. 24–25). Of special interest in Matthew is the nature of the kingdom of heaven and the church. His Jewish background no doubt influenced his interest in the community aspect of the Gospel.

Luke is the first volume of a two-part work which also includes Acts, the two intended as a carefully written review of the beginning and advance of the gospel until it had become a world faith. The author was the Gentile physician, Luke, Paul's traveling companion. He may have written from Rome, Corinth, Ephesus, Caesarea, or Antioch, and the date given is usually somewhere between A.D. 70 and 90. Luke is not only the longest Gospel, but with Acts comprises two sevenths of the entire New Testament. His has been called the Universal Gospel, the Gospel for everybody. Luke was fond of showing how Jesus sought to help the underdog—the poor, infirm, widow (or any woman in need), the Samaritan, or the Gentile. He stressed joy, cheerfulness, thanksgiving, prayer. But perhaps Luke's most distinctive contribution was his understanding that the gospel is for the whole world.

What he began to relate in his Gospel, he continued in Acts. In some ways it is unfortunate that John's Gospel is inserted between them, for Luke's purpose would be even plainer if Acts followed it in the canon. Acts is not the story of the apostles' work. They had a relatively small role in the continuing mission of Christ into all the world. Some of their names never even appear in Acts, and only Peter and John are reported as having been especially involved in evangelism. Acts is what its name implies—acts of God through the Holy Spirit in the church. These acts may be seen as a succession of breakthroughs which led the church out of the restricting, choking confines of legalism, provincialism, and racism to accept the universal nature of the gospel. To "go into all the world" was not a geographical but a personal instruction. The gospel could not be exclusive and be gospel. "Unhindered" is its key word, for Christ broke down the walls that divide men from one another. This is the message of Acts.

The Johannine Writings

Four New Testament writings belong to the writer whose name they bear—the Gospel of John and the three letters of John. It is thought by some authorities that the person who wrote these four did not write Revelation, because of a dissimilarity between them. Whether or not the apostle John wrote the Gospel and the letters is not clear. Although John 1:14; 21:24, and 1 John 1:1–4 say that the author was an eyewitness of the life of Jesus, it is possible that the documents came from a writer who learned what he recorded from that eyewitness. If John the apostle lived to the end of the first century A.D., the period reflected in these writings, he could be the author. There is solid tradition that he lived to a very old age in Ephesus, most commonly given as the place of writing. On the other hand, these could be a collection of the apostle's personal recollections which have been put together by an intimate disciple of the apostle known as John the Elder. There was such a man in the church at Ephesus, and it is observed that both 2 and 3 John are identified as from "the elder." If this is really the case, it would account for both the late date and the strong tradition that John the apostle is the source used by John the Elder. William Temple's conclusion is sound, however: "I regard as self-condemned any theory of authorship which fails to find a very close connection between the Gospel and the son of Zebedee [the Apostle John]." [3]

The differences between John's treatment of the gospel events and that of the Synoptics are extensive. It has been estimated that only 8 percent of his material is paralleled in any of the other three Gospels.[4] Some of John's distinctives are: (1) a lengthy Judean ministry of Jesus at the beginning of his career and three (rather than only one) Feasts of Passover; (2) long discourses but few parables; (3) the cleansing of the Temple at the beginning rather than at the end of his ministry; (4) the careful selection of seven miraculous events, which John called "signs," as evidence that proved Jesus' deity; (5) the Holy Spirit, "another Counselor," discourse of John 14–17; (6) washing the disciples' feet at the Last Supper rather than the installation of the Lord's Supper (John 13); (7) the emphasis upon "eternal life" as the supreme gift of Christ, whereas the Synoptics use the concept of the "kingdom of God" to describe the same state of redemption.

Yet it is easy to exaggerate these differences. The same "gospel" is reported in all the Gospels. The differences of approach and emphasis should not be allowed to obscure the common witness that all give to the person and work of Jesus as Christ and Lord. As our witness to Christ today is affected by the conditions to which the gospel needs to be addressed, so John's Gospel and Letters reflect the situation confronted by the church at the end of the first century: the widespread influence of gnosticism, threatening the purity of Christian doctrine; the conflict with Judaism and the need to clarify the relationship between Jew and Christian, both of whom relied upon the Old Testament; and the continuing influence of John the Baptist, especially around Ephesus, calling for a statement of the role of the Baptist as Forerunner to the Messiah. These are recurring emphases in John's writing.

Since early Christian history, John's has been known as "The Spiritual Gospel," because he not only reported a happening but saw beneath the actual event a deep spiritual lesson. One example will illustrate. When Jesus fed the five thousand, John reported this not only as a miraculous event of multiplying physical food but more importantly as the occasion of Christ's teaching that he is "the bread of life." John's Gospel comes alive when read from this understanding of what he purposed to do with his account of the gospel.

The Letters of Paul

Except for Romans, there are no formal treatises from Paul. His letters were responses to particular situations, usually having to do with problems in the churches he had helped to establish. They are letters in every sense of the word, following a nearly uniform pattern of naming himself as author, naming the recipient(s), giving a greeting which was followed by a word of thanksgiving (except for Galatians), discussing the matters which provoked the letter, and personal remarks such as greetings to friends, prayers on their behalf, and farewells.

In point of writing, the first of his letters were to the church at Thessalonica, and are a reflection of a pressing problem at the time Paul wrote, about A.D. 51. This was the question of the second coming of Christ and the end of the age. Some Christians had mistakenly believed that the end was imminent. When they saw their fellow Christians dying, they could not understand it because they had thought that Christ would return in their generation. Paul wrote to correct this erroneous idea, telling them that no human being has God's timetable, but that in the meantime every Christian has the obligation to be faithful and busy. The Thessalonian letters probably were written from Corinth, where Paul stayed for a year and a half, beginning about A.D. 49 or 50.

From Corinth he also may have written Galatians, a passionate appeal to the Christians of the Galatian churches not to succumb to the arguments of certain "Judaizing" Christians that they must accept Judaism as a Christian prerequisite. Paul's letter is a clarion call for Christian liberty: "For you were called to freedom, brethren; only do not use your freedom as an opportunity for the flesh" (Gal. 5:13,

RSV). Little wonder that Christians who opposed legalistic restrictions to their religion have found their inspiration in Galatians. Martin Luther wrote: "The Epistle to the Galatians is my epistle; I have betrothed myself to it; it is my wife." [5]

Paul's next letters in the New Testament were probably Corinthians, written from Ephesus during his three-year stay sometime about A.D. 55. It may be more accurate to call this "the Corinthian Correspondence," for there were at least three and probably four letters rather than the two we have. Paul's relationship with the church at Corinth was stormy. The city was a wicked seaport town in which the Christians as a "colony of heaven" were having a hard time living with one another and keeping the rottenness of their society from corrupting them. Paul wrote one letter before the one we know as 1 Corinthians, in which he appealed to them to eradicate such corruption from the church. In 1 Corinthians 5:9 he alluded to this earlier communication, and it is commonly believed that a part of this "lost letter" is preserved in 2 Corinthians 6:14 to 7:1, where it is apparently out of place. Read the context, and the logic of such a conclusion will be clear.

A little later Paul received a report (1 Cor. 1:11) that there was still trouble at Corinth, and he also received a letter from the church asking his advice about certain matters. This evoked the letter we call 1 Corinthians, in which he took up the problems one by one and dealt with them: divisions and dissension in the church (1:10 to 4:21); immorality (5:1–13; 6:12–20); lawsuits between members (6:1–11); marriage (chap. 7); food offered to idols (chaps. 8–10); problems of worship, such as the veiling of women and eating the Lord's Supper (chap. 11); spiritual gifts (chaps. 12–14); the resurrection (chap. 15). The letter concludes with greetings and thanksgiving (chap. 16).

Paul's letter was not well received in Corinth. Learning of it, he made a "painful visit" (2 Cor. 2:1, RSV) to Corinth. It accomplished no more than the letter had. Chagrined and hurt, he returned to Ephesus and wrote the church at Corinth exactly how he felt, sending it by Titus. What he wrote is likely our present 2 Corinthians 10–13. These four chapters reflect feelings nowhere else revealed in Paul's writings. But apparently they got the desired results. Paul, hearing nothing from Titus, became anxious and left Ephesus for Corinth. On the way, in Macedonia, he met Titus returning with heartwarming news. The Corinthians were penitent and wished to be reconciled with Paul. They realized that they had wronged him and asked his forgiveness. The great man was deeply moved and sat down and wrote them again. He said that he had written the other letter "out of much affliction and anguish of heart and with many tears, not to cause you pain but to let you know the abundant love that I have for you" (2 Cor. 2:4, RSV).

A gracious, tender outpouring of thanksgiving and appreciation follows. He was relieved and happy that the relationship was restored, and he asked them to complete the offering for the poor saints of Jerusalem so that when he arrived they would have it ready. This is 2 Corinthians 1–9.

He did come on to Corinth and according to Acts stayed three months before leaving for Jerusalem with the "collection for the saints." It was his last visit, for he was to be arrested in Jerusalem; but while staying there in Corinth, he wrote his letter to the Romans, whom he hoped shortly to visit.

Romans is the classic treatise on the nature of the gospel as justification by faith. It is the only "formal" letter we have from Paul. In it he set forth what he understood to be the tenets of our faith. His thought developed from a basic conviction expressed in a thematic statement in Romans 1:16–17: The gospel is not just a message, but an act of God's power through which all who commit themselves in trust to what God did in Christ may be saved. In this act God reveals his righteousness, his way of responding to man's lost condition; and this revelation is given to us only through faith —faith which is itself a gift from God.

From this statement of position, Paul elaborated his understanding of the gospel: (1) all men are under the universal sway of sin and death (1:18 to 3:20); (2) God has come to the rescue, and we may receive his aid through faith in what his grace has done to "justify" us, to treat us as righteous even though we are not (3:21 to 4:25); (3) there is a new life in Christ, a new dimension of living which calls us to "salvation," the living out of the life of justification (chaps. 5–8); (4) God is sovereign Lord of history and he is working his purpose out for all mankind, including Paul's own kinsmen, the Jews (chaps. 9–11); (5) God's righteousness in the Christian's life is expressed in ethical living (12:1 to 15:13). The letter concludes with a note about his hopes and plans to visit Rome and a series of personal greetings sent to individuals. In a more relaxed and thoughtful manner, Paul in Romans did what he had earlier done in Galatians—set forth the bases of Christian freedom, justification by grace through faith, ethical living as the product of grace rather than the means of it, and the call to Christian maturity.

The Prison Letters

After Romans was written, Paul left Corinth and returned to Jerusalem, where he was arrested, taken to Caesarea, and there remained for more than two years until sent to Rome as a result of his appeal for a review of his case by the emperor. Possibly in Caesarea, certainly in Rome, he wrote other letters. It is likely that there are four of these prison epistles—Philippians, Philemon, Colossians, and Ephesians.

The Philippian church, having heard of Paul's imprisonment, had sent a gift by Epaphroditus, who had become seriously ill. The church learned of his illness and was deeply concerned. Paul wrote to reassure them that their fellow church member had survived and would return to them. But he also wrote to thank them for their gift, a kindness they had shown him at least twice before (Phil. 4:15–16). In addition, he wished to allay their fears for his own welfare. What had happened to him had turned out for the good of the gospel: others were made bold by his courage; the gospel was reaching many who otherwise would not have heard it; and even some who disliked him were spurred on to preach more vigorously, even though they did it "from envy and rivalry" (1:15, RSV). He had not only wanted to report to them, but to warn them against legalists and Judaizers who would turn them from the gospel of grace, and against sensualists who abused Christian freedom to indulge their physical appetites. But the dominant note of this letter is joy. No fewer than sixteen times the words "joy" and "rejoice" occur. It is a song from prison.

Philemon is one of Paul's letters addressed to an individual. Its recipient was a certain Philemon of Colossae, a Christian through earlier contact with Paul (v. 19). He was the owner of a runaway slave, Onesimus, who also became a Christian when he met Paul in the city where the apostle was in prison. Onesimus, whose name means "useful," had been useful to Paul; but now Paul was sending him back to Philemon "no longer as a slave but more than a slave, as a beloved brother" (v. 16, RSV). Paul did not attack the institution of slavery. In Colossians, sent at the same time as the letter to Philemon, he urged slaves to be obedient to their masters and masters to treat slaves justly and fairly (Col. 3:22 to 4:1). We should not suppose that Paul was indifferent to injustice. Christians then lacked the power to abolish slavery. They could, however, deal with the problem of human relationships within the community of faith. Therefore, Paul would appeal to Philemon to receive Onesimus as a fellow Christian and to treat him as a brother.

Along with the letter to Philemon, Paul sent his letter to the church at Colossae, both carried by a Christian named Tychicus. This letter is a ringing affirmation of Jesus Christ as the full revelation of God. False teachers were seeking to introduce worship of angels and other intermediaries between God and man, reducing the central role of Christ. Some also sought to teach a form of legalism which promised merit with God for practicing asceticism. Against all such heresies Paul registered the strongest protest. Christ is all you need in order to know God, "for in him all the fulness of God was pleased to dwell" (Col. 1:19, RSV).

The language and thought of Ephesians have much in common with Colossians and make it appear likely that the two were written and sent, along with Philemon, at the same time. In the oldest Greek manuscripts of Ephesians, the words "at Ephesus" (1:1) do not appear. That and the fact that no personal greetings are included in this letter presumably addressed to the church where Paul had spent three years suggest that Ephesians is properly a "general" letter. This is to say, Paul sent the letter to be read in all of the churches of Asia Minor, inasmuch as it represents his mature reflection upon "the mystery of his [God's] will, according to his purpose which he set forth in Christ . . . to unite all things in him" (Eph. 1:9–10, RSV). That is the theme of the letter. Christ is our peace who has broken down the dividing wall of hostility to create one new humanity in himself (2:14–16). This worldwide outreach of the gospel of God's grace is expressed in and through his church, in which there are specific assignments (apostle, prophet, evangelist, pastor, and teacher); but every believer is a minister on mission under the lordship of Christ.

The Pastoral Letters

First and 2 Timothy and Titus, known as the Pastoral Epistles, all have introductions saying that they are letters from Paul to his children in the faith. They were accepted in the canon as his work. But they are quite unlike Paul's other letters in vocabulary and style, in their emphasis on good works, sound doctrine, and formal church organization (bishops and elders). The possible human explanation for these letters in their present form is that Paul wrote brief letters to his young protégés during the closing days of his life, telling them of his plans and encouraging them to stand fast in the faith. Then, sometime later, the letters may have been enlarged by a student and admirer of Paul.

Letters of Crisis

In some respects all New Testament letters are "crisis" documents. But as time passed, opposition from the state and the world became more severe; and crisis over doctrine became more acute. Heretical ideas threatened to corrupt the faith. It is possible to arrange some New Testament letters chronologically from the kind of crises they record. For example, 1 Peter should be dated early, perhaps in the early sixties. The letter indicates that the church faced severe trial, but not from persecution by the state. Indeed, Christians were reminded of their duty to pray for and obey state officials (2:13–17). Persecution was coming from popular dislike of Christians because of their opposition to paganism. It would be a "fiery ordeal" (RSV) (4:12–19; 5:6–11) and they were admonished to stand fast, to regard persecution as a test, and to "suffer as a Christian" (4:16).

Another of these "letters of crisis" is Hebrews. Its date is uncertain, but its author (now not believed to have been Paul) was at home in the Greek language. In fact, his Greek is some of the best in the New Testament. A very practical purpose motivated the writer—to strengthen the readers who have undergone and will again undergo severe trial. The man who wrote Hebrews was at home, not only in Greek, but also in Hebrew tradition. Upon the background of the Hebrew sacrificial system, he painted the picture of Christ as the great High Priest who in his death bore the sins of his people and now in his glory intercedes for them. In order to steel his readers to face persecution, he called the roll of the heroes and martyrs, and challenged them not only to have faith but also to be faithful.

One of the most controversial letters is James. Martin Luther, for whom Paul was the standard of Christian doctrine, publicly regretted that the letter of James had ever been included in the canon, because he believed that it rejects the doctrine of justification by faith. James seems to say that faith alone is inadequate to render a man acceptable to God: "You see that a man is justified by works and not by faith alone" (2:24, RSV). It is doubtful, however, that this is an attack on Paul. It is probably an attempt to correct a perversion of Paul's doctrine of faith that had crept into the church during the last years of the first century. There was a tendency to lose something of the Pauline sense of faith as commitment of life to Christ and to think of it more as acceptance of proper doctrine about Christ. Paul would have scorned that interpretation of faith as much as the writer of the letter of James did. This is mainly, then, a book of practical admonitions to such groups as the rich, the self-indulgent, the contentious, the talkative, the proud, the complaining, and the deceitful.

Two other brief New Testament letters reflecting crises of false doctrines are Jude and 2 Peter. Jude is a letter against heretics. The writer is "contending for the faith which was once for all delivered to the saints" (v. 3, RSV). It was likely written late in the first century. Second Peter is related to Jude. Many scholars feel that someone writing in the name of Peter used the material in Jude as the basis of his second chapter. He denounced false teachers who also practiced immorality, appealing to the righteousness of Christ and the example in the Old Testament of God's judgment upon wickedness (2:1–10). He concluded with a rebuke to those who use the fact that the second coming of Christ has not taken place as an excuse to scoff at the gospel, reminding them that God keeps his own timetable, and that his calling to his people is to be watchful and faithful. Second Peter probably was written early in the second century.

The book of Revelation was written by a Christian named John about the year AD. 95, while its author was in exile for his faith on a barren island called Patmos off the coast of Asia Minor. The Roman Government, under Domitian, was breathing fire and brimstone upon the church. John wrote to call Christians to stand firm in their faith in the face of suffering and death. In a message cloaked in symbolic language of visions and numbers, John portrays a great war in progress between the powers of evil (the dragon) and good (the Lamb, which is Christ). In heaven the war is over, the dragon defeated decisively through the sacrifice of the Lamb. The dragon (Satan) has been cast down to the earth where he continues to harass the church, using the beast (the Roman Empire) as his "front" or tool. The beast is the Roman Empire, waging war as the chief agent of Satan against the church. There can be no compromise with the dragon or the beast. The beast is doomed to destruction. Babylon (Rome) will fall.

Of special interest are the letters to the seven churches (chaps. 2–3), for in them are graphic portrayals of conditions of faithfulness and courage as well as of immorality, unfaithfulness, and lukewarmness. Also particularly fascinating is John's frequent use of the number seven, the symbol of perfection or completion. There are seven seals, seven trumpets, seven visions of the kingdom of the dragon, seven visions of the Son of man, seven bowls, seven visions of the fall of Babylon (Rome), and seven visions of the end.

Perhaps no book of the Bible has caused greater controversy and confusion. But no book of the Bible is more full of hope and faith in the ultimate triumph of God over the evil and folly of man.

This review has reminded us that the New Testament was written over a period of perhaps sixty to seventy-five years in response to particular needs in the church by men in varying places and circumstances and under the guidance of the Holy Spirit. Let us now turn to the exciting story of how these sixty-six books of the Old and New Testaments became the Book and how it has come down to us today.

---

[1] A. M. Hunter, *Introducing the New Testament* (Philadelphia: Westminster Press, 1946), p. 25.
[2] Vincent Taylor, *The Formation of the Gospel Tradition* (New York: St. Martin's Press, 1935), p. 175.
[3] William Temple, *Readings in St. John's Gospel* (New York: St. Martin's Press, 1963), p. xiv.
[4] Filson, *op. cit.*, p. 370.
[5] Hunter, *op. cit.*, p. 112.

CHAPTER NINE

How the Bible
Came to Us

One of the fascinating chapters in the history of the Bible is how its various "books," the work of many authors over a period of more than a thousand years, were gradually brought together and came to be regarded by the church as sacred and authoritative. Their preservation through centuries of copying and translation without their meaning being altered is also a part of this exciting story. It is a process of cumulative weight given to these particular religious writings among many similar ones, culminating in the canonization of those believed to be divinely inspired. It is a record of painstaking manuscript copying, careful translation, an incalculable amount of biblical study, and, in recent years, an abundance of corroborating and illuminating evidence from scientific research. This remarkable story will be briefly told, with the conviction that the Holy Spirit providentially guided the human process by which we got our Bible.

How the Old Testament Canon Developed

"Canon" is a transliteration of a Greek word which translates a Semitic word meaning "reed." The reed was one of man's earliest measuring instruments, and it is easy to see how the word could come to mean a rule, guide, pattern, or standard. As early as the third-century scholar Origen, the word "canon" was used to designate those religious books considered to be divinely inspired and, therefore, "the rule and guide of faith and conduct."

Christians inherited from Judaism a body of sacred literature, the Old Testament, which both Jew and Christian accepted as divinely inspired, although they differed in their view of its meaning. Christians believed that the Old Testament was given under the direction of God as a prelude to the coming of Christ, that its promises are fulfilled in him, and that its deepest meaning is found only in him. In the beginning, Christians had no other Scripture than the Old Testament. It had not always been regarded as Scripture. Before its present form most of it had been preserved and transmitted as oral records. Moreover, large segments of it are the result of centuries of accumulation of materials. In the Law, for example, we have not only the basic code of Moses but later expansions and elaborations needed to fit changing situations in the developing community of Israel. Therefore, many years might separate laws which stood side by side in the same code. This may be noted also in Psalms, a collection of poetry for use in worship, and in the wisdom sayings, such as are found in the book of Proverbs.

Further, it is helpful in understanding the significance of the Old Testament canon to realize that not all of the religious writings of Israel were accepted as Scripture. In fact, there is ample evidence of an abundance of such material which never was included in any canonical collection. (See Num. 21:14; Josh. 10:13; 2 Sam. 1:18; 1 Kings 11:41; 14:19,29 for Old Testament references to writings not included in the canon.)

One other clarifying observation is added. The Old Testament canon did not "drop from the sky" or suddenly appear with no previous history or meet with immediate and general acceptance as the official list of religious books which could be relied upon as sacred and authoritative Scripture. As a matter of fact, collections varied and those variations are still reflected in present-day Bibles. Sometime in the third and second centuries B.C., a translation of the Hebrew Scriptures was made into Greek for the benefit of the large number of Greek-speaking Jews in Egypt who no longer understood Hebrew. This famous translation was called the Septuagint. This is so named because, according to a tradition, seventy rabbis produced the translation in seventy days, each working independently and producing seventy identical Greek texts! (Actually the work was done by seventy-two men.) This is the version from which the New Testament writers, when citing the Old Testament, nearly always quoted. The obvious reason for their doing so is that they understood and wrote Greek rather than Hebrew, and so quoted from the Greek Old Testament.

Later, when Alexandrian Jews established a canon, they included all of the books of the Septuagint plus fourteen others called Apocrypha, which comes from a Greek word meaning "hidden" and reflects the anonymous character of the writings. Although Protestants, following the Hebrew canon, do not regard it as inspired, the Apocrypha is valued because its books were written about the intertestamental period, 200 B.C.-A.D. 100. The Roman Catholic Church, adopting the Alexandrian collection rather than the Hebrew canon, accepts the Apocrypha as canonical and includes it in its Bible.

The passage of time was a factor in canonization. Most of the Old Testament writings were canonized long after they were written. The process of canonization involved more than a gradual accumulation of reverence for certain books, however. Internal pressures such as the need for an authoritative body of religious instruction, caused by the Exile and the loss of the Temple as a rallying symbol in 587 B.C., hastened the process. So did such external threats to Israel's faith as the Hellenizing influence during the Greek and Maccabean periods. After all, when the Greeks banned the possession of Hebrew religious writings under penalty of death, it would tend to cause the Jews to decide which of their writings should be preserved even at the risk of death. Under such influences the canon crystallized.

The earliest biblical reference to a document having authority as the "book of the law" is in 2 Kings 22:8. This is the occasion in 621 B.C. of the discovery of the scroll by workmen making repairs on the Temple. It was taken to the high priest, Hilkiah, who read it to King Josiah. The king was moved by the commands of the book to advance the program of national reform which was already under way and to call the people to a renewal of their covenant relationship with God. This book, considered authoritative as the word of the Lord by Josiah and his associates, may have been the book of Deuteronomy.

During the exile in Babylon, the Jews carefully examined and

studied their religious literature. It served as a source of continuity
with the past and as a guide in the present for a people cut off from
their homeland. When the priest Ezra came to Jerusalem from Babylon in 428 B.C., he brought a book of law which had been accepted
in Babylon and which was made the basis for the reorganization of
the nation. This was no doubt the Torah, the first five books of our
Old Testament.

The next section of the Old Testament to become authoritative
was the prophetic literature. The Hebrews divided the prophetic
books differently from the way to which we are accustomed. They
designated as "Former Prophets," instead of historical writings, the
books of Joshua, Judges, 1 and 2 Samuel, and 1 and 2 Kings. This
was done because the prophets were deeply involved in the life of
the period covered by those books. The other section of Hebrew
prophetic literature was called "Latter Prophets" and included Isaiah,
Jeremiah, Ezekiel, and the Twelve (our Minor Prophets). It was
following the Exile that the prophetic writings came to be considered
Scripture.

The third section of Old Testament literature to be canonized was
the group known as the Writings. These included: Psalms, Proverbs,
Job, Song of Solomon, Ruth, Lamentations, Ecclesiastes, Esther,
Daniel, Ezra-Nehemiah, and 1 and 2 Chronicles. These books had
come to be regarded as Scripture by New Testament times.

Jewish controversies with Christians, who accepted the Hebrew
Scriptures but also used Christian writings, led to the limiting of the
canon for Jews. A group of Hebrew scholars meeting in Jamnia in
Palestine, A.D. 90–100, sought to establish the canon of accepted
Hebrew writings. It should be emphasized that this was not by any
means the only canonical council for Hebrew Scripture, nor were
its conclusions universally accepted.

However, the Old Testament canon was definitely fixed in Palestine by the end of the first century A.D., and it is the collection of
books accepted by Protestants as our Old Testament.

There is no question about the place of the Old Testament in the
thought of New Testament writers. Jesus often quoted the Scriptures,
and cited them as authoritative. "Thus it is written" was a familiar
introduction to the use of the Scriptures as an authority. Such respect
was given to all parts of the Old Testament, and from most of its
books there are either direct quotations or allusions in the New

Testament. Clearly Jesus loved the Scriptures and pointed men to them for guidance. When a scribe came to ask him about eternal life, he replied by referring him to the Scriptures: "What is written in the law?" (Luke 10:26). He chided Sadducees who questioned him about the resurrection: " 'You know neither the scriptures nor the power of God' " (Matt. 22:29, RSV). And to Jews who opposed him he said boldly, " 'You search the scriptures, because you think that in them you have eternal life; and it is they that bear witness to me' " (John 5:39, RSV).

The Language and Text of the Old Testament

Except for isolated verses, the Old Testament was written in Hebrew, which is a twenty-two letter language written and read from right to left. In the Hebrew text there were no vowels, since the alphabet has only consonants, and no punctuation. Vowels and punctuation were supplied by the reader, making possible an endless number of variations in reading. The text was originally written on scrolls (long rolls) of parchment, which were pieces of skin glued together, or of papyrus, which was woven into a sheet from fibers of an Egyptian plant. From about the third century A.D., manuscripts began to be put in "book" or leaf form, which was called a codex. There are obvious advantages in writing, handling, or reading material in this form.

Reproducing materials was slow and tedious. It might be done by a scribe copying directly from one manuscript to another scroll or codex, or by one scribe reading aloud to a group of scribes, each producing a copy by recording what he heard. The latter method was obviously faster but was also more likely to produce errors. Since scribes were human, errors were inevitable. These might be errors of the eye or ear in which the scribe misread the text or heard incorrectly, or a lapse in which a word or line was omitted. Occasionally there was an intentional change in the text (as, for example, scribal alteration of Hebrew names which incorporated the name of the despised Canaanite god, Baal). Once in a while a note, originally written on the margin of the page to explain some point in the text, would subsequently be included in the text itself.

Far from casting a shadow on the trustworthiness of the text, these minor variations between manuscripts reflect its overall reliability. They are also a tribute to the devotion of the scribes, called

Sopherim, "Men of the Book," who preserved a pure text from one generation to another, marking doubtful passages, making marginal notes about alternate readings, and dividing the text into sentences and sections for more convenient use. From about the beginning of the Christian era, another group of Jewish scholars continued the care of the Hebrew text. They were known as Masoretes, "Men of the Masora," or "fence," because they sought to build a careful fence about the Scriptures to protect them from any corruption. From the seventh to ninth centuries A.D., they added vowels and accents to the text to assure its standardization, for obviously changing the vowels supplied to a given set of consonants could produce a wide variation of meaning. Let the reader supply a vowel or vowels to the letters "r—d" for a simple illustration. They also counted and recorded the number of words in each section to assure that no additional words were inserted in the text.

Of course, there are no original manuscripts of any of the books of the Bible. In fact, the oldest complete Hebrew text of the Old Testament dates from A.D. 1008. Until 1947 there were only a few fragments of Hebrew texts dating earlier, and these were from the ninth century. The discovery of the famed Dead Sea scrolls has uncovered a large amount of valuable textual material, including a complete copy of the book of Isaiah dating from a time prior to the birth of Christ.

How the New Testament Canon Developed

As has been noted, the church already had a body of authoritative and sacred Scriptures, the Old Testament, when the New Testament canon was formed. More than that, it possessed the authority and leadership of the Holy Spirit. Yet despite these guides, it acknowledged the divine inspiration and authority of a collection of writings which it called "The New Covenant," or New Testament. Further, it interpreted the Old Testament by the New, not the New by the Old.

As in the case of the Old Testament canon, the books of the New Testament did not receive immediate recognition as inspired, although the process took a much shorter time. The letters of Paul may have been the first writings of our New Testament to appear, but they were not thought of as "holy writ" when they were first circulated. No reference is made to them, for example, in the Synoptic Gospels which were probably written between A.D. 65–90. But it is believed by many that the Revelation, appearing about A.D. 95, and the Gospel of John, dating about A.D. 100, show definite signs of familiarity with the Pauline letters. Evidently by that time these writings had been collected and were being circulated to all of the churches as being of more than particular and local interest. It is probable that not many years after the writing of John's Gospel it was combined with the Synoptics to form another "unit" of New Testament materials and, like the letters of Paul, began to be circulated among the churches. A reference to the letters of Paul in 2 Peter 3:15–17 indicates that by early second century they were looked upon by Christians as inspired.

As was true of Jewish writings, there were many Christian writings which were not canonized. It would be an error to assume that the writings finally included in the canon were the only valuable ones circulated in the early church. The material written about Jesus and his followers was voluminous. Much of it is pure fantasy; and some of the documents are quite heretical, while others make valuable contributions to our understanding of the church of the second century. Included in these are gospels, epistles, apocalypses, and acts. How did the church sort out the authentic from the spurious? Again, the passage of time provided opportunity for the sifting of materials; and the books which were to receive recognition as Scripture "proved themselves worthy." Councils which adopted official canons did not formulate the canon so much as recognize what was already in existence by common usage in the churches.

It is impossible to date the beginning of the New Testament canon, but the activity of the Christian Gnostic, Marcion, about A.D. 140 must have hastened the process. Marcion, wishing to establish Christianity as an anti-Jewish, nonmaterial, "spiritual" religion, published his own canon consisting only of an expurgated edition of Luke plus ten letters of Paul. It was perhaps to counteract the influence of such heretics that the second-century church began to publish lists of the books to be considered authoritative. Certain books, notably Hebrews, James, and 2 Peter, were omitted from some of these early lists, while other writings such as the Epistle of Barnabas, Shepherd of Hermas, and Revelation of Peter were often included. In the long run, the books which we have in the New Testament were accepted as Scripture, and others were not.

Among the earliest canonical lists is the "Muratorian Canon," named after its discoverer in Milan in 1740. This list dates from about A.D. 170 and begins with a broken sentence which seems to refer to Mark. (It is assumed that Matthew has been lost from the beginning of the document.) It names the other New Testament books except James, Hebrews, and the Epistles of Peter. A Revelation of Peter is also mentioned, but it is indicated that some would not permit it to be read in the churches. The first list identical with present-day copies of the New Testament is found in a letter issued at Easter, A.D. 367, by Bishop Athanasius of Alexandria. It should not be supposed, however, that because this conclusion had been reached in Alexandria by A.D. 367, it was reached everywhere at that time. In some places it may have been earlier, and in others it was certainly later. Canonization was a process, not a decision made by a council of bishops.

The Language and Text of the New Testament

As is generally known, the New Testament was written in koiné, or "common," Greek. It was the vernacular, the language of commerce, rather than the classic language of Plato and Aristotle. Until the nineteenth century, the nature of New Testament Greek was the subject of a great deal of speculation. Some people advanced the idea that the Holy Spirit had given the New Testament writers a special variety of Greek for these inspired writings. Then papyri discoveries in Egypt revealed that the New Testament writers had simply used the spoken language of everyday communication.

New Testament wording also reflected extensive use of the ideas and language from the Old Testament. Many New Testament words and ideas are illumined and enriched by knowledge of the Old Testament. Having always been exposed to the New Testament, it is difficult for us to appreciate how much of its meaning roots in the Old Testament. The name Jesus, for example, is Greek and corresponds to the Hebrew word for Joshua, meaning saviour. "Christ" is a Greek word meaning the anointed, and its Hebrew counterpart is "messiah." The Greek word for Lord is *kyrios*, and it is used to translate the Hebrew word "Yahweh," the name for God in the Old Testament. So when the disciples called Jesus "Lord," they meant more than that he was their superior or master. They meant to identify him with God. Even these few observations and illustrations indicate that study of the language greatly enriches the understanding of the meaning of the New Testament.

Greek manuscripts of the New Testament were of two varieties: *uncial,* that is, written in capital letters; and *minuscule,* written in small, cursive (running) letters often joined together. The uncials predominated until the ninth century A.D., after which the minuscules became more common. No uncials appear after the eleventh century. One would suppose that, because of being earlier, the uncial manuscripts would be the more valuable. Generally that is true, but not always. The rapid, widespread growth of Christianity resulted in the dissemination of the Scriptures from several centers of Christian activity. The manuscripts circulated thus tended to fall into "families," that is, to descend from some particular "line" of manuscripts. Manuscripts were made by copying other manuscripts. Therefore, if a certain alteration occurred in the text of a given manuscript, or if an error occurred in copying, these alterations tended to be passed down in the subsequent "family" of manuscripts. This would mean that some manuscripts might be more accurate than others which were older.

Among the principal families of texts are: the Alexandrian, which originated in Alexandria, Egypt; the Byzantine, which originated in the late third century around Antioch in Syria; the Western, which probably originated in North Africa and was soon translated into Latin; the Syriac, which became the basis of the authorized Bible of the Syrian church; and the Caesarean, believed to have come from Caesarea and to be as early as perhaps the second century A.D.

Specific manuscripts, belonging to one or the other of the "families," are considered by biblical scholars as having great weight in deciding what is the most accurate text. For example, the *Codex Sinaiticus* is a middle fourth century manuscript of Alexandrian text and is one of the most important witnesses. So also are the *Codex Alexandrinus,* a Byzantine text of the early fifth century, and the *Codex Vaticanus,* a fourth century text of the Alexandrian family. There are literally thousands of New Testament Greek manuscripts, either in part or whole; and we are indebted beyond measure to dedicated scholars who have given themselves to the effort to arrive at an accurate text and to throw all possible light on the meaning of the Scriptures.

Two other sources for the study of the text of the Bible should be cited. One is the various ancient versions. Even before the New Testament era, the Old Testament was translated out of Hebrew into other languages for the benefit of Jews scattered all over the Roman world who were no longer able to read the language of their religion. The same condition produced translations of the entire Bible from Greek into other languages as the gospel advanced across the world: Latin for the people of the West and Africa; Syriac when the gospel spread to Syria; Coptic for Egyptians; and subsequently Armenian, Ethiopic, Georgian, and Arabic. In the last of the fourth century, Jerome, a Latin Bible scholar, was commissioned by the Pope to revise the earlier Latin version in order to provide a standard translation. Athough the results were at first controversial, Jerome's Vulgate, meaning "common" or "vernacular," became for nearly fifteen hundred years the official Bible for the Roman Church.

The other important source of information about the text of the Bible was the Church Fathers, leaders of the church in early centuries who often quoted the Scriptures in their writings and sermons. These quotations are of obvious priceless value in helping to determine the accuracy of the text.

It should be remembered that although an incalculable amount of time has been devoted to biblical research, and although thousands of divergencies have been discovered in the thousands of manuscripts now available to be studied, the vast majority of them involve inconsequential matters such as alternative spellings, order of words, and additions or omission of words or phrases which do not change the meaning. How can biblical scholars determine whether omissions, additions, and transferences took place in a text? By comparing it with older and better texts. For example, the King James Version, based on late texts, quotes Jesus as saying in the Sermon on the Mount that if we give alms, pray, and fast "in secret," "thy Father which seeth in secret shall reward thee *openly*" (Matt. 6:4,6, 18). It turns out that the better Greek texts do not have the word "openly." We can only surmise that a copyist along the way sought to "improve" the text by adding "openly," perhaps concluding that Jesus meant to say that good deeds done in secret would be openly rewarded. Or "openly" may have been added inadvertently through a mental lapse, or it may once have been a word written in the margin which some later copyist included in the text.

We owe much to biblical research. It not only has put us in touch with a more accurate text of what the original writings said, but it has thrown an enormous amount of light upon their meaning. In no case has it given cause for doubt as to the authority and authenticity of the Bible.

The English Bible

Christianity came to the British Isles with Roman soldiers, but it was not until the seventh century, under the leadership of a Roman monk named Augustine, that rapid growth of Christianity in England took place. During the Anglo-Saxon period some portions of the Bible, notably Psalms and the Gospels, were translated out of the Latin Vulgate into the vernacular. However, the first complete English translation of the Bible was made from the Vulgate by John Wycliffe and others between 1378 and 1384. Believing that the Scriptures and not the Pope were the authority of the church and that every person, whether a clergyman or not, should be able to read them in his own language, Wycliffe and his followers issued many copies of two English translations in manuscript—of which one hundred and eighty remain.

It should be remembered that Wycliffe's work was done from Jerome's Vulgate, but the first English translation of the New Testament from the original Greek was done on the Continent in 1525 by an exile, William Tyndale. He also translated portions of the Old Testament, using the Hebrew Old Testament text of the Masoretes. Before he could complete his work, Tyndale was martyred for the "heresy" of putting the Bible in the vernacular. Tyndale is especially important in the history of the English Bible because he used Greek manuscripts, although they were late ones providing a poor text. Furthermore, Tyndale's lively, direct, and vivid style was to influence subsequent English translations, particularly the King James Version. It has been estimated that one third of the actual wording of the King James Version comes from Tyndale.[1]

In 1535, the first complete English Bible to be printed came from the press. This edition was the work of Myles Coverdale, but most of the text came from Tyndale's translation. In response to a request from Thomas Cromwell, vicegerent of King Henry VIII, for an authorized Bible, Coverdale issued a revised edition of his and other English translations. This was published in 1539 and became known as the Great Bible because of the large size of its pages. The psalms from the Great Bible are still in use in the Book of Common Prayer.

The next important translation of the English Bible was published in Geneva in 1560 by a group of Protestants exiled from England during the reign of Henry VIII's Catholic daughter, Queen Mary. The Geneva Bible was one of the most popular English translations, about two hundred editions being issued between 1560 and 1630. It was the Bible of Shakespeare, John Bunyan, and the Pilgrim Fathers. Its scholarship was quite good for the day. The translators worked from Hebrew and Greek manuscripts and also made use of various previous translations. One other Protestant translation prior to the King James Version, the Bishops' Bible, should be mentioned. This translation was published in England in 1568 to counteract the influence of the Geneva Bible, which was considered by the bishops of the Church of England as unsuited for use in their services. The Bishops' Bible was largely a revision of the Great Bible.

During the turmoil of the Reformation in England, Roman Catholic scholars exiled in France provided an English translation for the use of English-speaking Catholics. The New Testament was done at Rheims, France, in 1582 and was called the Rheims Version. The Old Testament was published in 1609–10 at Douai, using the Vulgate. Later, revised and combined with the New Testament translation, it became the approved English version for Catholics in America in 1810 and is known as the Douai Version.

The King James, or Authorized, Version was the last and best known of the English translations during the Reformation period. There was a lively interest in having a standard, readable, vernacular Bible at the beginning of the seventeenth century. A great deal of Hebrew and Greek scholarship had already developed; and the English language itself was flourishing from the work of men like Shakespeare, Marlowe, and Spenser. Many Puritans believed that a new translation was needed to replace the ones done in the reigns of Henry VIII and Edward VI. Accordingly, at the direction of King James I, an impressive group of about fifty scholars began the work in 1604. Nearly three years were consumed in translating and editing the work, the scholars divided into six companies—three to translate the Old Testament, two the New Testament, and one the Apocrypha. Each man was given an assignment, and his translation was checked and approved by his company, then sent to the other companies for their suggestions and approval. Previous translations, particularly Tyndale's, Coverdale's, the Geneva Bible, and the Bishops' Bible, were used. In addition, the translators used the Greek and Hebrew texts and other language versions—Latin, Syrian, French, Italian, German. The manuscript was bought by the king's printer, Robert Barker, for 3,500 pounds, and first made its appearance in 1611.

The Authorized Version was not everywhere well received, however. The Pilgrims in America, for instance, rejected it in favor of the earlier Geneva Bible. Gradually, however, it gained favor; and although it was never officially designated as the "Authorized Version," for multitudes of English-speaking Christians during the past centuries it has been "The Holy Bible," and any move to revise it has met with fierce opposition from some quarters. What is not realized by people who oppose newer translations is that the King James Version, like others before it, was itself a revision of earlier work. The translators, foreseeing that some would object to what they had done in making a new translation, wrote in a preface called, "The Translators to the Reader," as follows: "Was there ever anything projected, that savored any way of newness or renewing, but the same endured many a storm of gainsaying or opposition?" [2] It is also important to remember that the King James Version went through numerous revisions itself before 1769 when it took the final form in which we know it today.

As the King James Version represented only a chapter, although an important one, in the story of the English Bible, so the nineteenth and twentieth centuries witnessed the writing of further history of biblical study. Scholars continued to feel the need of a better translation. One of the factors influencing such thinking was the enormous amount of research in textual studies, particularly of the Greek New Testament. The Old Testament text is based upon Hebrew manuscripts carefully copied by the Masoretes from earlier Hebrew manuscripts, which were then destroyed. Recent discoveries of Old Testament manuscripts, such as those found among the Dead Sea scrolls, confirm the accuracy of the Jewish scribes.

But there was wide variation in Greek New Testament manuscripts because there was no one center from which manuscripts came. Today in the hands of biblical scholars are more than forty-five hundred manuscripts or fragments of manuscripts of the Greek Testament. With an abundance of evidence on hand, it is singularly impressive that no serious doctrinal difference is reflected in best Greek texts. Indeed, we may join a contemporary New Testament scholar in affirming that "no future finds will alter in any essential the text of our Greek Testament. There are indeed numerous minor variations between manuscripts, and scholars weigh them carefully. But these are relatively unimportant." [3] But while the text is not likely to be materially altered, the tools of biblical research are continually being used to bring about a clearer understanding of the text.

Another reason for continual revision of translations is that the language into which we translate is continually changing. The language of the King James Version is stately and beautiful, but some of it is archaic and not clearly understood. One Bible scholar has pointed out that more than three hundred examples of words used in the King James Version mean something substantially different from their current meaning.[4] Among the common ones are: "to prevent," used in the King James Version to mean to go before; "to let," meaning to hinder; "comprehend," in the sense of overcome; "conversation" to mean conduct; and "communicate" to mean share. Inasmuch as the purpose of a translation is to make a faithful rendering of the text in the most understandable language, rather than obscuring the meaning, it seems self-evident that fresh translations will continue to be needed.

In England a revision of the King James Version was issued in 1885. It was called the English Revised Version and was mainly the work of English scholars, although an American group also worked on the project with the agreement that recommendations made by the Americans would be given serious consideration and that all their suggestions not used would be included in an appendix. The Americans agreed on their part that they would not publish a competitive revision for at least fourteen years after the publication of the English Revised Version. Subsequently, in 1901 the American Standard Version was published. It was the result of the work of the American committee which had worked on the English Revised Version, plus additional research done in the interim. Both English and American Revisions were based on important advances in biblical research; but it was generally conceded that both were too mechanical, too tied to the literal translation of the Greek or Hebrew words of the text, and did not "come across" in the style of present-day English.

The Revised Standard Version represents a monumental amount of biblical scholarship. The New Testament was published in 1946 and the Old Testament in 1952. It has been severely criticized as being designed to cast doubt upon the unique place of Jesus Christ as Son of God, but this criticism is of doubtful validity. The translation has proved itself to be quite a good and fair one. In 1961, the New Testament part of the New English Bible was published. As the Revised Standard Version sought to improve the American Standard Version, so the New English Bible is a work of English scholars seeking to revise the English Revised Version by putting the text into accurate and contemporary language. The New Testament translation has received wide acclaim and acceptance.

Of course, there are numerous individual efforts at translation, some good and others of indifferent quality. Two that have received popular support are really more nearly paraphrases than translations, but they illuminate the text in many places. These are Moffatt's translation of the Bible and J. B. Phillips' translation of the New Testament. The New American Standard Bible is an effort by the Lockman Foundation to renew and improve the American Standard Version. *Good News for Modern Man: The New Testament in Today's English Version,* an American Bible Society project, has met with unprecedented public interest. Even more recently, the Tyndale House, Publishers, has offered the public a compilation of their paraphrased translation of the Bible under the title *The Living Bible Paraphrased.* Many Bible lovers have responded to this publication with enthusiastic acceptance.

The Value of Archaeology

In the search for the meaning of the text of the Bible, a vast amount of information brought to light through archaeology has been of great assistance. While archaeology should not be thought of as a means of proving the truth of the Bible, it is a fact that archaeological finds have again and again confirmed biblical references. A few examples are: (1) the Siloam inscription cut into the wall of a tunnel to celebrate its completion by King Hezekiah's workers in the eighth century B.C., bringing water into the city of Jerusalem, an event described in 2 Kings 20 and 2 Chronicles 32; (2) the Moabite Stone, a ninth century B.C. slab telling of the domination of Moab by King Omri of Israel; (3) the Black Obelisk of Shalmaneser III, an Assyrian monument containing the only known likeness of a king of Israel, showing King Jehu paying tribute to Shalmaneser III, the Assyrian; and (4) the Amarna Tablets, a group of tablets in Babylonian cuneiform but found in Egypt and telling of conditions in Palestine and Syria in the early fourteenth century B.C., a century or so before the Exodus.

These examples are only a few of those available, but they illustrate the value of archaeology in illuminating words, customs, places, and even the names of persons referred to in the Bible. Archaeology has proved to be one of the valuable tools used by biblical scholars to make it more nearly possible to recover the context in which the Bible was written so that its meaning may be more clearly understood.

---

[1] Edgar V. McKnight, *Opening the Bible* (Nashville: Broadman Press, 1967), p. 83.

[2] Quoted from D. Winton Thomas and others, *The Bible Today* (New York: Harper and Row, 1955), p. 146.

[3] Floyd V. Filson, "The Study of the New Testament," *Protestant Thought in the Twentieth Century,* Arnold S. Nash, ed. (New York: The Macmillan Co., 1951), p. 51.

[4] McKnight, *op. cit.,* p. 98.

CHAPTER TEN

The Bible Speaks
to Today

In this INTRODUCTION TO THE BIBLE, we have observed the nature
of the Book and the nature of God's speaking through the Book in
revelation and inspiration. We have scanned the "people and places"
of both Old and New Testaments and have examined the circumstances in which the books were written. In the last chapter, the
story of how the Bible came to us through canonization, copying,
and translation was briefly told. Among the many questions that remain, one presses for an answer: What is the message of the Bible,
what is it saying? Does it have a central theme, a thread running
through it, or is it only an assortment of religious writings gathered
from widely separated times and places? Does it point us to the
meaning of life, or is it only a collection of pious observations
about life's mystery? Is it the story of things that happened in time
and place, even though the things it reports are extraordinary in nature; or is it only an anthology of quaint myths believed by our
primitive ancestors but having at best only academic interest to space-
age people?

The Unity of the Bible

No, the Bible is not an assortment of religious writings, a collection of pious observations, or an anthology of myths. It is a history,

yet it is more than history. It is history seen and understood from the perspective of commitment to God. It is faith-history. It is history that is concerned not only with fact but with meaning of the fact. It always represents the two as related. The message of the Bible is the recitation of God's mighty acts, not done in heaven but on earth. These mighty acts began with creation, and the Bible's testimony concerning it gives witness to three pivotal affirmations: (1) the universe exists because God is and wills the universe to exist; (2) man is unique in the creation, having been made with the capacity for communion with his Maker; (3) all that God made is good, and it is his purpose to redeem it from the evil which was brought by man's rebellion.

The theme of redemption runs through the Bible like a crimson thread once ran through ropes of the British navy to identify them as authentic. And this redemption takes place in history with God as the principal fashioner. The world of events is his workshop. Through the life of a particular people of his own choosing—a people whose father was Abraham, a man of faith—God's mighty acts of redemption were done. It was God who took them into Egypt and God who led them out in the Exodus. It was God who gave the law at Sinai through Moses and God who brought them to the Promised Land and made them a nation. It was God who raised up the prophets and who allowed his people to go into bondage because of their sins. It was God who delivered them through Cyrus the Persian and prepared the way for the coming of the Messiah. "But when the time had fully come, God sent forth his Son, born of woman [i.e., within humanity], born under the law [i.e., within Israel's covenant relationship with God], to redeem those who were under the law, so that we might receive adoption as sons" (Gal. 4:4–5, RSV). It was God who sent forth his Son.

What God began at creation and completed at Calvary, that is, our redemption, he repeats in every life where the miracle of re-creation in Christ is allowed to happen. The Bible is the record of what God has done and is doing to redeem us. But it is also the prediction of what is to come. It looks backward to creation and to Calvary; it looks forward to the end of history and the consummation. It is seen, then, that "redemptive history" proceeds through three stages. In the old covenant, the promise of redemption was given, embodied in the hope of a Messiah but veiled by the future.

When "the time had fully come," the second stage took place. It was the stage of fulfilment. Christ has come, the veil is removed, and the nature of God's righteous love is fully revealed. But a third stage awaits—it is the consummation. The Bible can only give witness to it in faith, as the church sees it from afar and pushes on toward the end of history and the time when " 'the kingdom of the world has become the kingdom of our Lord and of his Christ, and he shall reign for ever and ever' " (Rev. 11:15, RSV).[1]

The point is that the story of redemption belongs to the entire Bible, not simply to one or the other of the Testaments. Christ did not come "out of nowhere." He came into a historical situation. This is precisely the point of the incarnation. Christ was no archangel suddenly swooping down to flit about on wings that never touched our common humanity. That was what the Docetists, who denied his humanity, wished to make of him. It is little wonder that their most prominent representative in the church, Marcion, tried to get rid of the Old Testament! But the Old Testament is indispensable to the Christian because it bears witness to the historical context of Christ and points forward to him. As the risen Lord walked with the two disciples along the road to Emmaus, "beginning with Moses and all the prophets, he interpreted to them in all the scriptures the things concerning himself" (Luke 24:27, RSV).

To be sure, the Old Testament has meaning apart from the New Testament. It would ill behoove Christians to deny that the Scriptures (Old Testament) have meaning to the Jew. Moreover, they have meaning as history quite separate from their New Testament implications. For instance, one of the most familiar messianic verses in Isaiah says, "Behold, a virgin shall conceive, and bear a son, and shall call his name Immanuel" (7:14). It would be difficult for a Christian to read this verse without concluding, as Matthew did when he wrote his Gospel, that the words are perfectly fulfilled in Jesus Christ (Matt. 1:23). But this is not to say that Isaiah's words had no meaning other than the messianic one, and that for more than seven centuries they remained an enigma. No, the words were spoken in the form of reassurance to faithless King Ahaz of Judah that if he would trust God and not run to Assyria for aid against his enemies, God would deliver him. The Old Testament often has such a "double meaning," speaking to its first hearers and pointing to the future, particularly when it speaks of some future "Day of the Lord," a mighty manifestation of God's coming to men. Christians are convinced that these predictive sayings find their fulfilment in Christ.

So, there is continuity between the Old and New Testaments, even though the Old Testament has a meaning all its own. That continuity lies in the fact that the Old Testament is fulfilled in the New. At one stage, the people cried to God in a vivid image, "O that thou wouldst rend the heavens and come down" (Isa. 64:1, RSV). The New Testament claim is that the cry has been answered. God has come to men, since men could not get to God. "He has come in the only way they could possibly understand, as a person like themselves." [2]

But the continuity between the two Testaments is seen not only in the New Testament's fulfilment of the Old, but in the light which the Old Testament throws on the New. It is the same God who speaks in both, and he does not speak out of two sides of his mouth. Much of the New Testament is illuminated by the Old. For example, we understand what Paul meant when he referred to Christ as "the last Adam" (1 Cor. 15:45), because we know what the Old Testament means by the first Adam. Marred by deliberate sin, Adam is man as he was meant to be but is not. Adam is what we all are. Christ is what God intended us to be. As the first Adam spoiled God's work, the last Adam makes its restoration possible and is himself the model for it. Thus, as the New Testament fulfils the Old, the Old Testament enriches the meaning of the New.

However, it is important in this discussion of the unity of the Bible not to overlook the unique and absolutely new thing which has happened in Christ. We are not to conclude that because there is demonstrable continuity between the Testaments there is no discontinuity. There is radical newness. It was not idle talk that Paul made when he spoke of the "scandal of the cross" (1 Cor. 1). Let us not forget that Jesus gave the most serious offense to the very people most deeply devoted to the Scriptures. They would not accept him; he was too different. Something new, cataclysmic, happened in Christ. Though the Old Testament Law and Prophets bear witness to his coming, he is the unique, unrepeatable gift of God. The Old Testament could foresee his coming; it could not foresee his glory, for "he reflects the glory of God and bears the very stamp of his nature" (Heb. 1:3, RSV). Nothing like that ever happened, before or since.

These words put it plainly: "Christ comes, not merely as the greatest in a series of prophets, but as the Son, as the author of a new age, as the head of a new humanity." [3]

The Central Message of the Bible

Come now to the specific content of the theme which unifies the Old and New Testaments. It is the theme of redemption, what has been called "salvation history." The term suggests the nature of the biblical message: It is the story of what God has done in and through history for man and for his salvation. In the chapters of this small book, we have sought to review that history. We need now to re-emphasize that its meaning from the Christian perspective is that it is the story of God's redemptive work among us.

The climax of the story is the coming of his Son, Jesus Christ. In him the prophecy has been fulfilled, and the New Age has arrived. In the death of Christ, God has demonstrated the depth of his love for man. But the cross represents more than a demonstration. It is the breaking of the grip of evil; it is the doom of sin. By the way of the cross, man finds God leading him home. It is not the cross alone, however, that describes the mighty redeeming act of God in Christ. It is also Jesus' resurrection. The two were never separated in New Testament preaching of the gospel. Jesus died to redeem man from his sins; but God raised him from the dead, the vindication and glorious proof that the power of sin had been overcome. And now the believer, having experienced this "new creation" of himself in Christ (2 Cor. 5:17), walks in newness of life. He makes no pretense to sinlessness (Rom. 7:15–20; 1 John 1:8–10), but he will not habitually sin and he will not take sinning lightly (Rom. 6:1–2). Moreover, he looks forward to the completion of himself as well as to fulfilment of the purpose of God for all in the world to come.

This, put in many contexts and said in many ways, is the central message of the Bible. Some would raise a question as to whether or not we Christians do not read into the Old Testament a good deal of salvation history that is not there. We do not think so. For example, it is impossible for a Christian to read the moving passages about the Suffering Servant, particularly those of Isaiah 52:13 to 53:12, without hearing the nails driven through our Lord's hands and feet and into the wooden beam—"He was wounded for our transgressions."

But he was more than the Suffering Servant. The fulness of the meaning of Christ defies description, and those who knew him and were elected by God to describe him to us held up various pictures to our spiritual gaze. One of the most common titles is the "Son of man." Jesus himself found great meaning in the title, which we might assume was a way of identifying him with our humanity; but there is a great deal more to it than that, and here again the Old Testament is the source of the meaning. The title is used in Daniel 7:13 and others and also in the noncanonical book of Enoch with which Jesus was no doubt familiar, and it had the meaning of God's special representative.

While the Gospels, especially Mark, accented the title Son of man, they also used other descriptive titles of him—one is "Son of God." (See Mark 1:1; 8:29; 14:61 for examples.) Another is "Christ," or "Christ, the Son of God." Two familiar examples of this designation are Peter's confession of Christ reported in Matthew 16:16 and John's statement of purpose for writing his Gospel (John 20:31). The writer of Hebrews, with his orientation of Temple and ritual observances, sees the Old Testament figure of Melchizedek, priest-king of Salem (Gen. 14), as a type of Christ, the great High Priest who makes the perfect atonement for man's sin.

Perhaps the closest thing to a "confession of faith" in the New Testament is the simple declaration: "Jesus is Lord." It has already been observed that for the Christians to call him "Lord" meant more than that he was their "Commander in Chief." It was to identify him with God, whose Old Testament name is translated LORD. To say, "Jesus is the Lord" (1 Cor. 12:3) or "Jesus Christ is Lord" (Phil. 2:11) was to make a faith commitment to him as the source of all meaning and of one's hope for life eternal. It was, in short, to make a Christian confession.

Perhaps nothing in the New Testament more plainly puts the matter of Jesus' identity than the transfiguration. There he was on the Mount, with Moses and Elijah (law and prophets) having disappeared, standing alone. He was the fulfilment of all law and prophets. He did not come to set them aside. " 'Think not that I have come to abolish the law and the prophets; I have come . . . to fulfil them' " (Matt. 5:17, RSV). He is the heart of the Bible, for he embodies—incarnates, "enfleshes"—God's purpose of redemption.

But what of the Movement which God has brought into being,

the people who own him as their Lord, in the days of both the Old and New Covenants? This is part of the message of redemption, and this part may be examined by looking at the meaning of four words.

Election—Covenant—Remnant—Community

Throughout the Bible there is the continual note of God's guidance of his people. This is not to suggest a "closed system" in which the providence of God is turned into a godless fatalism. Man's freedom must always be placed beside God's purpose in history, for without freedom man would be a puppet, not man. Without freedom neither sin nor forgiveness could exist. Without freedom man's wrong choices are not choices, and to offer him forgiveness for something he has not chosen to do makes no sense.

Nonetheless, God ordained; God chose. Probably the one word that best expresses God's choosing of Israel is "election." God selected the instruments through which his saving purpose was to be expressed. He chose Abraham from the sons of Terah; he chose Jacob over Esau; he chose Joseph, bringing him to Egypt for his own purpose (Gen. 50:20). He chose Israel to be his people, delivered them from Egypt, prepared them in the wilderness and at Sinai, and gave them the Promised Land. At the proper time he sent Christ, his elected instrument, for the saving of men (1 Peter 2:4,6). Christ was "the stone which was rejected by the builders" (RSV), but which God made to be the cornerstone (Acts 4:11). Christ in turn chose a people to come out from the world, to be with him, and to be sent out to preach and have authority to cast out demons (Mark 3:15). This was the nucleus of the church, "the called out." As Israel had sensed herself to be the elect, the chosen one, so the church saw herself as the New Israel, the elect of God in Christ, chosen by him and called out to be the bearer of his redemptive message to the world.

The "chosenness" of Israel was established by a covenant and rested upon God's faithfulness to his people in keeping the covenant relationship. Israel believed herself to be a covenant people. Never did a rainbow hang in the sky but that God's covenant promise after the Deluge was recalled. Never was the rite of circumcision performed on the happy occasion of the birth of a man-child but that Israel remembered the covenant of God with Abraham. Never was the Passover meal served, with its salt water and hyssop, unleavened bread, wine, and the paschal lamb, without rehearsing again the timeless events of God's deliverance of his people from Egyptian bondage. Never did a father hear his children's recitation of the law, speak of it to them in his house or along the way, or attach small reminders of it to his doorposts or wrists or forehead without remembering what it meant to have a covenant relationship with God (Deut. 6:7–9).

The covenant of God was not an ordinary one, for it was not an agreement between equals, reached by bargaining. The covenant was a gift and a demand. God made promises to Israel, but he also made certain requirements. He kept his part of the covenant, but Israel did not. The prophets continually recalled Israel to her agreement, but she kept breaking it. One of the prophets, Jeremiah, foresaw a time when God would "rewrite the contract," making it an internal one, written upon the hearts of the people (Jer. 31:31–34).

This God did! In Jesus Christ he rewrote the contract. He put his covenant in men's hearts, calling them to a higher obedience than the law. And as Jesus sat in the upper room with his disciples on the last night before the cross, he said to them: " 'This cup is the new covenant [agreement] in my blood' " (1 Cor. 11:25, RSV). The writer of Hebrews, with his continual reference to the relationship between the Old and New Covenants, put it plainly: "For if that first covenant had been faultless, there would have been no occasion for a second" (Heb. 8:7, RSV). Christians understand themselves to be people of the covenant.

That is neither a boast nor an apology. Election did not mean special privilege but special responsibility. Unfortunately, the people of the covenant commonly chose to interpret their relationship with God to mean special privilege. It turned their religion into an arrogant racism and exclusiveness. Jesus condemned that attitude so strongly that to get rid of him they nailed him to the cross. That did not stop him, however. It only served as the means of bringing his purpose to fulfilment. But some of the elect of the New Covenant did not do much better. They could not put aside their exclusiveness until the Holy Spirit, through men like Stephen, Philip, Barnabas, and Paul, broke down the dividing walls of hostility that separated man and made the covenant the possession of all who had faith.

"Remnant" is another great biblical word connected with God's purpose of redemption through the Chosen People. Few people enjoy being "leftovers," for our social instinct recoils at separation from others. Yet God is always separating the wheat from the chaff, the sheep from the goats, the brave warriors of Gideon's band from the fearful multitudes, the faithful from the unfaithful. This is what is meant by remnant. As the Bible sees it, the remnant has always been a minority, but in it lay the hope of the future. Think how often God relied upon a remnant. Noah was a remnant. Abraham, chosen to leave Haran for Canaan, was a remnant. The ten faithful men vainly sought by Abraham to save Sodom from God's righteous indignation represent the remnant. Caleb and Joshua, the two faithful spies out of the twelve sent into Canaan, represent the remnant. So does the lonely prophet Micaiah, standing firm against King Ahab's four hundred false prophet "yes-men." And then there was Elijah who found that the remnant numbered 6,999 more than he had supposed, since he had imagined that he alone of the faithful was left. In Isaiah's day, things looked grim for Judah and so the prophet expressed his faith in the future of God's people by naming one of his children "A remnant shall return." His son may have been no better pleased with his name than some of us are with ours, but the name his father gave him expressed one of the deepest convictions of the Bible. God never leaves himself without a witness. There is always a new shoot out of the old stump.

The church in the New Testament found the figure of the remnant suited to its understanding of its role in the world. It recalled the words of Jesus about the hardness of the hearts of the people of the world and took courage. Jesus had spoken in parables with the same result that Isaiah had observed among his contemporaries: " 'You shall indeed hear but never understand, and you shall indeed see but never perceive. For this people's heart has grown dull, and their ears are heavy of hearing, and their eyes they have closed, lest they should perceive with their eyes, and hear with their ears, and understand with their heart, and turn for me to heal them' " (Matt. 13:14–15, RSV). The parables were not given to conceal the truth, but to reveal it so plainly that hearers could not evade its demands or avoid responding to it. But the response could be negative, and continually to say no brought such hardness of heart and deafness of ear and blindness of eye that saying yes became humanly impossible. The mystery of the remnant is that they have said yes to God in Christ, while the rest of the world goes on saying no.

But the remnant, who are bound in a covenant relationship with

Christ, are not a bundle of sticks which happen to be tied together by the same string, or a collection of isolated individuals related only by an accident like occupants of a lifeboat. They are a community which has both vertical and horizontal dimensions of relationship. The vertical dimension is one of forgiveness and communion with God. The horizontal dimension is not a tax levied against the value of the vertical relationship, but an integral part of it and a way of both experiencing and expressing it. The horizontal dimension of the community of Christ is love for one's brother (1 John 3:10b–18; 4: 7–12,19–21). In this dual relationship the church is sustained.

The Bible and the Church

To speak of the church is to talk about more than the local institution. At the same time, we should be wary of the notion of church as a kind of fuzzy abstraction that never quite gets into focus. The church is "both . . . and," not "either . . . or." God called a visible community to be his own people. As Israel was only a family of Semites apart from God's choosing her, so the church gets its meaning, not from the illustrious company in it (1 Cor. 1:26–30), but from God's choosing it. Jesus Christ did not leave a book, a creed, a system of thought, an assortment of "rules for gracious living," but a visible community, a company of people "with ascertainable names and addresses." [4]

There are at least four marks of the New Testament church. First, *faith in Christ is the constitutive element* (Mark 1:14; John 3:14–16; 5:24; 6:28–29; Acts 2:44; 4:32; 16:31; 15:10–11). The last reference listed has to do with the controversy over whether or not Gentiles would be required to become Jews in order to be Christians. Peter made a clear case for faith as the constitutive element of the church. God, he said, had chosen Abraham for faith; God had chosen Peter and had prepared Cornelius the centurion for faith; God had provided his own witness (the Holy Spirit) and had cleansed the hearts of the Gentile believers by faith alone. It goes without saying that Paul's entire ministry was a testimony to justification by faith. (Read Rom. 1:16–17; Eph. 2:8–9 as examples.) We must conclude that the church exists only where the gospel is preached, heard, and responded to in repentance and faith.

But there is more to the church. It is *Christ's visible expression of his life in the world*. To become a believer is not to remain an isolationist, but to be incorporated—embodied. When he came, he chose twelve to "be with him" (Mark 3:14–15). He did not tell them everything (John 16:12), but he gave himself to them. Their mission was not to make an idea, a doctrine, or a proposition known, but to make *him* known. Paul's understanding of the church clearly points to it as the body of Christ. The Lord's Supper was a symbolic sharing in the body of Christ (1 Cor. 11:20–29). The church is indeed Christ's body (1 Cor. 12:12–27; Eph. 1:22–23; 4:15–16; 5:23). The church is God's temple (1 Cor. 3:16; 2 Cor. 6:14–16; Eph. 2:11–22). The personal life of the believer is incorporated into the body of Christ (1 Cor. 6:15). No fewer than one hundred and sixty-four times Paul speaks of being "in Christ" or some variation of the expression, indicating the mystical union of believers with the life of Christ. This is more than an individual and personal matter —Christ in you and you in Christ. It is that, but it is more. It is that Christ continues to be known through the church, his body.

Furthermore, *the church is the community of the Holy Spirit.* Where is the church? It is where the Holy Spirit is present with power. In the upper room Jesus talked to his disciples about his departure and the coming of the Holy Spirit. Remember that at the time of John's writing, the church was looking back on some seventy years of experience. John was not writing about things predicted, but things experienced. Read these five "Paraclete" sayings: John 14:1–17,26; 15:26–27; 16:7–8,12–15. In essence Jesus said to them: "I will not leave you orphaned. Another just like myself, except that he has no human body for the world to lay hands upon, will come to be with you forever. He will continue my work of teaching, comforting, rebuking, and judging." When Peter accosted Ananias and Sapphira for their deceit (Acts 5), he said: "You have not deceived the church; you have lied to the Holy Spirit." If one asks, "Where is the church?" the answer must be in part, "It is where the Holy Spirit is experienced in power."

Finally, *the church is where there is true fellowship, community in Christ.* This fellowship is best expressed in the Greek word *koinonia,* and it more nearly connotes "family" than anything else. What are the marks of a good family? Sharing, love, respect, loyalty, acceptance, freedom to be a person, responsibility—these are some qualities of a good family. Cross out the word "family" and write "church." The list should still apply. That is the Bible's understanding of it.

How does the church, which is all four of these things—constituted by faith, the body of Christ, the community of the Holy Spirit, and a true family—express what it is by the way it lives?

How the Church Lives

The church sustains its life through the worship of God in Christ. Worship in the community of faith in Christ as Lord is the joyous adoration of God as he has come to man in the historic event of his Son and continues to reveal himself and minister to us through his Holy Spirit in the church. It is the penitent confession of our sin and the welcoming assurance of pardon. It is the faithful voicing of intercession and petition to One who "knows what you need before you ask him" (Matt. 6:8, RSV). It is humble commitment. Worship is the life of the church and of the believer. It is no optional matter for either. Nothing serves so well to check splintering, unbiblical individualism or dogmatic propositions of faith as does worship.

The church is a community of learning. Turn back to John 14:26 and read again what Jesus said about the teaching ministry of the Holy Spirit. God has revealed himself fully in Christ, but our understanding of the revelation is at best partial. Further, as life unfolds before our eyes in the actual living of it, the implications and applications of the gospel become more meaningful. Christ is adequate for every new situation; he has a word for every occasion. But we have to hear his word afresh as it speaks to every new condition. This is the teaching ministry of the church, and the Holy Spirit is the teacher.

The church exists as a community of forgiveness. The church is called by its Lord to be a community in which the people of God may experience again and again the sense of being forgiven. (Read Matt. 18:15-20.) Then is the church a polite company of stuffy, starched "saints"? No, it is a community of the forgiven through whom the reality of God's forgiveness continues to be made manifest.

The church is a community of sharing. Throughout the Bible the corporate nature of the people of God is insisted upon. "And all who believed were together [of one accord] and had all things in common" (Acts 2:44, RSV). This "holding in common" was not alone a mutuality of sympathy and concern; it was expressed in the sharing of goods. "And they sold their possessions and goods and distributed them to all, as any had need" (Acts 2:45, RSV). James reprimanded those who suppose that faith may exist in a spiritual vacuum and chided pious well-wishing for one in need when the word is unaccompanied by deeds of sharing (James 2:14–17). Paul broadened the base of sharing even further to include mutual responsibility to support one another in time of temptation and failure (Gal. 6:1–3).

The church lives by being a community of witnesses. Indeed, all that it is (as expressed in the four aspects previously mentioned) is witness. Witness is not simply going on tours for Christ. It is essentially being an exhibit, a demonstration to the world, of what one has experienced in Christ and being this in the world, not removed from it. The church is a piece of the world, not a foreign substance in the world. It is a piece of the world which God in Christ has reclaimed and redeemed and made a base of operations for himself and his kingdom. As a base of operations and an exhibit of redemption, the church is God's instrument. What is the great "mystery" of God which now has been made plain in the gospel? It is this: "that *through the church* the manifold wisdom of God might now be made known" (Eph. 3:10, RSV).

The church lives by participating in God's purposes. What are his goals? What is he doing through his redemptive mission, his "plan of the ages" which began before the worlds were formed, which was embodied in Israel's history, came to a climax in Jesus Christ, and is now continued through the Holy Spirit in the church? His objectives appear to be three, two of which we now see and the third we may only anticipate.

One purpose is the reconciliation of all things in himself through Christ. What is "the mystery of his will, according to his purpose which he set forth in Christ"? It is "to unite all things in him" (Eph. 1:9–10, RSV). This is Paul's theme in Ephesians, and it was the burning passion of his ministry. A sundered, split, divided humanity, at war with itself, victim of its own fratricide and suicide, is to find wholeness in Christ. That is God's objective, and it is the church's privilege to participate in it. The way in which God has brought his work of reconciliation about is eloquently put in Ephesians 2:13–16. He who is our peace has taken the warring factions within man and between men and has healed them, making both one, breaking down the dividing wall of hostility. The result is the creation in himself of "one new man," one new humanity, thus making peace. A new breed in Christ has appeared, one that does not perpetuate the old hostilities, prejudices, and wars. In Christ, mutual destruction has been replaced by mutual construction. This is no superficial camaraderie or civic club "togetherness." Only a new humanity will suffice to heal the deep sore of our division. Where is the new breed? The church exists only where this "new breed" is found.

God's objective is also the realization of the full potential of all his creation. And just as we see, though imperfectly, the work of reconciliation, so also we see in part the work of fulfilment. The biblical view of sin is that it has had disastrous results: to man himself (Gen. 3:7); to man's relationship with God (Gen. 3:8–10); to man's relationship with his fellowman (Gen. 3:12); to nature (Gen. 3:16–17); and to God's purpose for his life (Gen. 3:19). The biblical view of redemption is that it is precisely these disastrous results with which God is concerned and about which he has done something remedial in his Son, Jesus Christ. In Colossians 1:15–22, Paul embraced both of these objectives of God in his thought and said that the purpose of Christ's coming was: "to reconcile to himself all things, . . . making peace by the blood of his cross" (1:20, RSV); and "to present you holy and blameless and irreproachable before him" (1:22, RSV).

John understood that God's intention for us is fulfilment; and although we are God's children now as much as we shall ever be, "it does not yet appear what we shall be, but we know that when he appears we shall be like him, for we shall see him as he is" (1 John 3:2, RSV). What else could Paul have envisioned in the immortal words, "For now we see in a mirror dimly, but then face to face. Now I know in part; then I shall understand fully, even as I have been fully understood" (1 Cor. 13:12, RSV)?

It is self-evident, however, that neither objective has been reached. Both of these goals, reconciliation and fulfilment, are already realized in Christ; but they are not completed in us, nor can they be, until the end, the consummation and Christ's return. The goals must be kept within the perspective of the church's hope in Christ, knowing that their full achievement awaits the culmination of history by his return. Paul's understanding of this will help ours: "We rejoice in our hope of sharing the glory of God. More than that, we rejoice in our sufferings, knowing that suffering produces endurance, and endurance produces character, and character produces hope, and hope does not disappoint us, because God's love has been poured into our hearts through the Holy Spirit" (Rom. 5:2–5, RSV). The hope is "realized" only in prospect; but it is not vain hope, for the Christian has the down payment, the earnest money of what is to be. The guarantee is the presence of the Holy Spirit.

We have no encouragement from the Scriptures to suppose that things are going to get better and better in this world. There is no doctrine of gradualism in the Bible. Rather, we may only view the goals through faith and labor for them with hope. As Paul also said cogently: "Now hope that is seen is not hope" (Rom. 8:24, RSV). Jesus' parable of the tares is a clear example of the biblical teaching concerning the doctrine of hope beyond history (Matt. 13:24,36–43). The tares and wheat are growing up together, each becoming more firmly rooted and stronger, until the harvest. Then the separation will come. So it will be with evil and good. The tares will not be rooted out. They are growing, but so is the wheat. One day comes the harvest. That is the Christian hope for the realization of both reconciliation and fulfilment. It is John's "new heaven and a new earth," the first heaven and the first earth having passed away (Rev. 21:1).

The church lives by being servant. This is the role of her Lord. Isaiah of the Exile saw him as the Suffering Servant. No words in the Scriptures more succinctly put Jesus' understanding of his work than these: " 'For the Son of man also came not to be served but to serve, and to give his life as a ransom for many' " (Mark 10:45, RSV). In the world, greatness is measured in terms of how many servants one can command; in the kingdom, greatness is measured in terms of how many others one serves (Matt. 20:20–28). The church is not a monarch, moving in stately elegance through the world, displaying its wealth and power. When the church is church, she is the servant of the world.

The church lives as a pilgrim people. The summons of God is always forward. So it was when God summoned Abraham from Ur of the Chaldees. So it was with Israel in the wilderness, where doubt and self-pity caused confusion and wandering which only ended when a new generation of greater faith was raised up. So Paul understood the meaning of his own personal pilgrimage (Phil. 3:8–14). How can the pilgrimage be made more appealing to us than it is in the words of the writer of Hebrews, as he calls us to "run with perseverance the race that is set before us, looking to Jesus the pioneer and perfecter of our faith" (Heb. 12:1–2, RSV)? We "can't go home again," as tempting as it is to try. Peter's wishing to "make three booths" and stay on the mountain with Christ in the transfiguration is a continual fantasy of the church (Mark 9:2–8). But we cannot institutionalize our insights, revelations, and deliverances. That has been the cause of the church's failure again and again. The story of the church is the story of pilgrimage. It is the passing of one barrier after another, always led forward by the Holy Spirit. Philip preached to Samaritans and to an Ethiopian, Peter to Cornelius, and Paul to pagan Gentiles. And on the widening circle of the church's mission outreach, the Holy Spirit puts its approval with power. The church does not have a mission; it is a mission. It is only a church when it is on pilgrimage asking always, "Where does the Holy Spirit lead now?"

How the Bible Speaks to Us

We near the end of the journey. There is a unity to the Bible; it speaks with one voice, the voice of God through the voices of men. The voices do not all speak with equal clarity, but they all speak one message. It is the word of redemption. It is redemption looked forward to in the Old Testament, fulfilled in the coming of Christ in the New, and to be consummated with his second coming at the end of history. But the message has never been spoken in a vacuum; always it has been through a community, the people of the covenant, a remnant. In Christ the community has become a New Israel under the New Covenant. It is the church, constituted by faith to be the body of Christ, animated by the Holy Spirit, and living as a community of worship, learning, sharing, forgiveness, and witness. The church lives also by participating in God's objectives of reconciliation, fulfilment, and consummation. The church is a servant always on pilgrimage.

This, it is our belief, is something of the message of the Bible. But how does this "come across" to us? How does God speak to me through the Bible in a manner different from the inspiration of good music, a fine sermon, or a well-written book? Is it that the Bible raises the perennial questions that have perplexed and troubled man?

"If a man die, shall he live again?" (Job 14:14)

"Am I my brother's keeper?" (Gen. 4:9)

"Why are you cast down, O my soul?" (Psalm 42:5, RSV)

"Why does the way of the wicked prosper?" (Jer. 12:1, RSV)

"Is there no balm in Gilead?" (Jer. 8:22)

" 'What do you think of the Christ?' " (Matt. 22:42, RSV)

" 'Who are you, Lord?' " (Acts 9:5, RSV)

" 'What shall I do, Lord?' " (Acts 22:10, RSV)

The experiences of the Bible are ours. But all literature that really speaks to us is only a page out of life. There must be other reasons why the Bible continues to speak uniquely to men's hearts and minds.

The Bible puts us in touch with the historic events in which God's redemptive work has been done. Throughout this course we have emphasized the crucial significance of the historical records. The Bible is not only a collection of religious truths; it is also the communication of a message. The message is about things that have happened which have changed man's life on this planet. It is a message which man could not hear in any other way. The Bible is relevant to us, then, because it tells how God has intervened on man's behalf at certain, concrete points in history. That intervention becomes a living reality in the present when the message about it comes to man and is received in faith. The Bible is the indispensable starting point, the place of entry to faith in Christ. To be sure, the work of Christ would be a reality without the Bible, but the Bible is the sacred repository of the record. We need the record, not only for the purpose of proclaiming the gospel, but for the correction of our proclamation of it.

But there is something more here than a record like the official weights housed in the Bureau of Standards, an invariable basis of measurement. The Bible is not simply a biography from the reading of which one may draw inspiration and guidance for living. The Bible is a living Word through which God speaks to our present condition. The Word speaks to us, not just by example or precept, not just by inference or implication. Its light on our condition is not a pale reflection from the events and people of which it speaks. It is not a secondhand word coming to us, or an echo from the word spoken in the days it reports. The Bible is a direct line to us. The testimony of an endless line of witnesses is that if a man comes reverently and in faith to the Bible, not as a spectator but as a participant—he finds himself and his situation being spoken to. Thus the encounter of God with man is being continuously reenacted. The historic Saviour of

whom the Bible speaks becomes a living reality, and we cry with
Thomas, "My Lord and my God." Nothing less was God's purpose
in giving us the Bible.

---

[1] Nygren, *op. cit.*, p. 31.
[2] Brown, *op. cit.*, p. 46.
[3] Nygren, *op. cit.*, pp. 12–13.
[4] Lesslie Newbigin, *The Household of God* (New York: Friendship Press,
1953), p. 21.

Personal
Learning
Activities

Chapter 1

1. What is the significance of the terms "Old Testament" and "New Testament"?
2. List three examples of the renewal of the covenant between God and Israel.
3. Explain in a few sentences why Roman Catholic Bibles include books not accepted by Protestants as Scripture.
4. Define "miracle" as the Bible uses it.
5. List three types of literature that appear in the Bible.

Chapter 2

1. Give a basic definition of "revelation."
2. What is meant by this statement: "Jesus Christ is 'the end of fragments' "?
3. In what ways has God revealed himself other than in the events recorded in the Bible?
4. Define "inspiration." How is this different from revelation?
5. Why do we need the Bible if we have Jesus Christ as our Saviour and Guide?

Chapter 3

1. What are the characteristics of the area in which the biblical

events took place which caused it to be called the "Fertile Crescent"?

2. How did the geography of Palestine affect the development of Israel?

3. Of what larger racial group migrating into the Fertile Crescent was the family of Abraham?

4. What historical event in Egypt coincided with Joseph's rise to power?

Chapter 4

1. Trace in a sentence or two the major campaigns of the conquest of Canaan by Israel under Joshua.

2. What was the role of the Judges in Israel's history?

3. List some of the major characters of this chapter and identify them.

4. What is the meaning of "prophet"?

5. What were some of the effects of the Exile upon the religion of Israel?

Chapter 5

1. What are the consequences of sin as reported in the Genesis account of the fall of Adam and Eve?

2. What was the original title of the book of Numbers and how was the title changed?

3. Compare the prophecies of Amos and Hosea.

4. Why was Jeremiah so unpopular during most of his career?

5. List three examples of Wisdom Literature in the Old Testament.

Chapter 6

1. List five characteristics of life in Palestine in the time of Jesus.

2. List the three major annual religious festivals of the Jews and indicate the reason for celebrating each.

3. Name the four major religious parties of the Jews and indicate the primary interest of each.

4. Explain briefly what Jesus meant by the kingdom of God.

5. Why did Jesus enter Jerusalem riding upon a donkey, cleanse the Temple, and teach daily during the week preceding his arrest and crucifixion?

Chapter 7

1. How do the Gospels relate the work of Jesus Christ and the work of the Holy Spirit?

2. What probably happened to the large Jewish element in the first-century church?
3. Briefly outline the life of Paul, including his background, up to the time he went on his mission journey with Barnabas.
4. What was the nature of the controversy which led to the decision reported in Acts 15? Was this decision a compromise by Paul? Explain the reason for answering yes or no.
5. Why are the years A.D. 65–100 often called "the obscure decades," and why is this period crucially important in the study of the New Testament?

Chapter 8

1. Why are Matthew, Mark, and Luke called the Synoptic Gospels?
2. List four differences between John's treatment of the gospel and that of the Synoptics.
3. What is commonly believed were Paul's earliest letters in the New Testament, when were they written, and what is their chief concern?
4. Give an outline of the major arguments of the letter to the Romans.
5. When was the Revelation written and what is its major theme?

Chapter 9

1. What does "canon" mean?
2. When was the Old Testament canon as we know it fixed?
3. Identify: codex, uncial, Masoretes, Muratorian Fragment.
4. Why is Marcion of interest to students of the Bible?
5. Explain why some Greek manuscripts of the New Testament are considered more valuable than others.
6. Why has it seemed necessary through the centuries to continue the study and translation of the Scriptures?

Chapter 10

1. What is the central theme of the Bible?
2. Explain the meaning of "election" and "remnant."
3. List four distinctives of the New Testament church.
4. List five ways in which the church, as seen in the New Testament, fulfils its purpose and mission.
5. Tell in a few sentences how you think the Bible speaks to us today.

From the Author to the Teacher

Chapter 1

A worthy objective in teaching this chapter would be to lead students really to "see" the Bible, to examine its contents and the relationships which exist between the Old and New Testaments and between the books in the Bible. Emphasize the meaning of "testament" as covenant. Point out the wonder of the Bible's "unity in diversity," that is, the central theme of redemption found throughout this collection of religious writings that were gathered from many sources across more than ten centuries. Use the Bible itself to identify types of literature in it: the stories of the primordial and prehistoric times of Genesis 1–11; the historical narratives of Samuel-Kings; the poetry of the Psalms; the legal and liturgical regulations of Leviticus;

Editor's Note: These chapter by chapter suggestions have been prepared by the author to help the teacher grasp more clearly the central ideas conveyed in each chapter. Dr. Johnson has also prepared a reading list for each chapter. (Listing of these books does not imply endorsement of their total contents by the author or publisher.) This section of the book contains a list of suggested audiovisual aids and a bibliography. These were prepared by Adeline DeWitt and Richard Kornmeyer of the Church Library Department.

the "philosophical" Wisdom Literature of Ecclesiastes or Job; the "preaching" of the prophetic writings such as Amos; the "sermons" in Acts; the symbolic and visionary writings of Daniel or Revelation; and the "down-to-earth" situational writing of the letters in the New Testament. Help the students to see that these various writings are "flesh and blood" material bearing the divine imprint and carrying within them the common mark of God's redemptive work.

Stress this chapter's emphasis upon the Bible as the record of God's revelation of himself through his people and supremely through his Son (which view was adopted by the 1963 meeting of the Southern Baptist Convention). Point out that this record is not mere reporting of historical event, but the interpretation of the meaning of event through the eye of faith.

Carefully study the section on the Bible and science, being sure that no impression is given that the Bible is not reliable because it is not a book of science. Be sure to make clear the fact that the biblical meaning of miracle is the intervention of God in the affairs of man— whether within or above the operation of natural law—to achieve his purpose, and that it is not simply any happening which does not have a natural explanation.

Suggested further reading:

Farmer, Herbert H. "The Bible: Its Significance and Authority," *The Interpreter's Bible*. Nashville: Abingdon Press, 1952, I, 3–31.

Neil, William. *The Rediscovery of the Bible*. London: Hodder and Stoughton, 1954, pp. 9–26, 65–98.

Richardson, Alan. *The Bible in the Age of Science*. Philadelphia: The Westminster Press, 1961, pp. 9–31.

Rowley, H. H. *The Unity of the Bible*. Philadelphia: The Westminster Press, 1955, pp. 15–37.

Chapter 2

It is of utmost importance to the understanding of this chapter that you discuss fully the concept of the Bible as "the record of God's revelation." Help students see that the expression in no sense detracts from the authority of the Scriptures. Rather, it points to the Bible's own view that God has revealed himself through what happened to his people and supremely through his Son. Revelation is God's self-disclosure, not man's discovery of God. Revelation took place in time and place, that is, in a historical context. Show how Christ is the full revelation, "the end of fragments," and that one may see this and still fully appreciate other religions. Do not fail to exalt Jesus Christ; he is the criterion by whom all Scripture is measured.

Help students to see that it is not necessary to espouse a mechanical, tape-recorder view of inspiration in order to maintain a reverent and thoroughly biblical view of inspiration. Point out that the Bible remains as a necessary corrective of our private and partial understanding of the nature of the gospel.

Suggested further reading:

Brown, Robert McAfee. *The Bible Speaks to You*. Philadelphia: The Westminster Press, 1955, pp. 39–49.

McKnight, Edgar V. *Opening the Bible*. Nashville: Broadman Press, 1967, pp. 11–16.

Nygren, Anders. *The Significance of the Bible for the Church*. Philadelphia: Fortress Press, 1963, pp. 1–11.

Chapter 3

Make good use of the two maps in the book and wall maps if available. Try to help students get the "feel" of real people living in real situations. Explain that we proceed from the conviction that God chose the time and place, not from the notion that the time and place shaped the religion of Israel. Nevertheless, the geography, topography, climate, and times chosen by God for his people influenced their lives.

If it is possible for the teacher to locate resource materials, it will be most helpful to enrich the necessarily sketchy outline of the ancient history of Israel given here by reading one or more of the following:

Bright, John. *A History of Israel*. Philadelphia: The Westminster Press, 1959, pp. 17–93.

Buttrick, George Arthur. (ed.). *The Interpreter's Bible*. Nashville: Abingdon Press, 1952, I, 232–275.

Oesterley, W. O. E. *A History of Israel*. New York: Oxford University Press, 1932, I, 3–64.

Robinson, H. Wheeler. *The History of Israel*. Naperville, Ill.: Alec R. Allenson, Inc., pp. 11–38.

Chapter 4

The review of Israel's history from the conquest of Canaan through the return from exile in Babylon is a huge undertaking to be accomplished only by telescoping long periods of time. Nonetheless, it need

not resemble a motion picture of a panorama taken so rapidly that
the entire scene looks like a continuous blur. To prevent this, con-
serve time by moving rapidly from one period to another, but stop
and examine in some detail certain eras of Israel's history. It is doubtful that a chronological chart of the kings of Israel and Judah would
be crucially important in this kind of study, but seek to give students
a broad perspective of what happened. Then "dig down" at specific
points and seek to interpret the people and events which dominated
that period. Work hard at doing what the Bible does, that is, making
its people real people and not cardboard characters.

Suggested further reading:

Anderson, Bernhard W. *The Unfolding Drama of the Bible*. New
York: Association Press, 1957, pp. 34–76.

Buttrick, George Arthur. (ed.). *The Interpreter's Bible*. Nashville:
Abingdon Press, 1952, I, 275–291.

Flanders, H. J., Crapps, R. W., and Smith, D. A. *People of the
Covenant*. New York: The Ronald Press Co., 1963, pp. 155–441.

Robinson, H. Wheeler. *The History of Israel*. Naperville, Ill.: Alec
R. Allenson, Inc., pp. 38–165.

Chapter 5

Students will especially need their own Bibles for the study of this
chapter, for its purpose is to give a concise summary of the contents,
context, and general period of each of the books or sections of the
Bible. Carefully distinguish between what can be established as fact
and what is conclusion based upon evidence but without absolute
verification. Help the class to see the relationship between historical
events and the era in which the books were written and the subject
matter of the books themselves. Occasionally, as in the case of Jonah,
the setting of the story is in an earlier time, and it is used to teach an
important truth about God in the era in which the book is written.

Perhaps a chronological chart of the books of the Bible in the
order of their writing can be useful here, together with another column
showing events in Israel or Judah and elsewhere, provided it is clearly
understood that in some cases we must make an "educated guess." It
is not a conclusion without evidence, however.

Stress the role and message of the prophets. Also, show how the
prophets represent different times and situations in Israel's history.

Suggested further reading:

Buttrick, George Arthur. (ed.). *The Interpreter's Bible*. Nashville: Abingdon Press, 1952, I, 175–219.

James, Fleming. *Personalities of the Old Testament*. New York: Charles Scribner's Sons, 1939.

Robinson, H. Wheeler. *The Cross in the Old Testament*. Naperville, Ill.: Alec R. Allenson, Inc., 1955.

Robinson, H. Wheeler. *The Old Testament: Its Making and Meaning*. London: Hodder and Stoughton, 1937.

Chapter 6

Important to the study of the coming of Christ is the understanding of the historical setting into which he came. Such an understanding gives meaning to much of the conflict which existed between him and such groups as the Pharisees and Sadducees. Seek to make real the kind of life in which Jesus grew up in Palestine so that students can "feel" their way back into the situation in which he lived. Show how the chief Jewish sects were proposing to deal with the problem of preserving Judaism. Explain that Jesus did not come in a "vacuum," but that there was a preparation and expectation about his coming. Let students talk about the life and teachings of Jesus, but lead them to examine the reasons why the New Testament put so much emphasis upon his death and resurrection.

Suggested further reading:

Beck, Dwight Marion. *Through the Gospel to Jesus*. New York: Harper & Row, 1954, pp. 3–29.

Buttrick, George Arthur. (ed.). *The Interpreter's Bible*. Nashville: Abingdon Press, 1952, VII, 75–154.

Filson, Floyd V. *A New Testament History*. Philadelphia: The Westminster Press, 1964, pp. 63–150.

Chapter 7

A map of the Mediterranean world of the first century is almost indispensable for the teaching of this chapter. Show people where it happened. Be sure you understand what was happening—a struggle for the emancipation of the gospel from bonds of nationalism, culture and race, and religious tradition. The Holy Spirit is seen in the New Testament church to be leading it to accept the universal implications of the gospel of God's redemptive work in Christ. The action in the Acts comes alive when seen from this perspective.

Note particularly the section on "The Obscure Decades," these being important because much of the New Testament appeared during this period and the church began to undergo changes which led to more formal and ecclesiastical polity. Do not be afraid to get back into the first century and be honest, but do not claim to know more than we do.

Suggested further reading:

Filson, Floyd V. *A New Testament History*. Philadelphia: The Westminster Press, 1964, pp. 151–394.

Stagg, Frank. *The Book of Acts*. Nashville: Broadman Press, 1955. This book is basic. Read it!

Chapter 8

Here you need your New Testament at hand as you study and teach. This is an opportunity to make an important contribution to the student's understanding and appreciation of the New Testament by showing him how it came to be. As has been suggested in an editor's note in the text, it is impossible to be certain of the precise order in which the various books of the New Testament were written. But we can make a reliable broad outline of their order, and when we do, their unified witness to the gospel becomes more meaningful.

Neither gloss over nor exaggerate difficult problems arising from the study of the New Testament books. To do the first is to lose the respect of people who want to know; to do the second is to major on minors, waste time, and miss the breathtaking wonder of the good news. Do not let a fly buzzing around in the car cause all the occupants to miss the grandeur and beauty of a day's journey to the mountains.

Let Paul, Peter, and James be the real men they were. Stained-glass saints may be pretty in church windows, but they do not come from the Bible. Help people understand that New Testament characters were involved in real life situations, that a crucial struggle between conscientious men is reported in Acts 15, for example, and that only the leadership of the Holy Spirit saved the church from being turned into a narrow sectarian movement.

Make as one of the aims of the study of this chapter an understanding of the primary thrust or thought of each book. People will have a new appreciation of Galatians, for example, if they know what Paul was saying and why.

Suggested further reading:

Beck, Dwight Marion. *Through the Gospels to Jesus*. New York: Harper & Row, 1954, pp. 33–68.

Hunter, A. M. *Introducing the New Testament*. New York: The Westminster Press, 1945.

Chapter 9

Here is an opportunity to dispel some of the fog of misunderstanding about the Bible that has clouded the minds of many people who love and revere it. Let us not yield one degree of our commitment to the truth of revelation and inspiration, while leading students to a knowledge of the long process by which the Bible came to us. This intriguing story of canonization, copying, and translation gives us a deeper appreciation of the unique worth of the Scriptures.

Give particular attention to the history of the English Bible. Because this is the Bible most of us know and love, we need to be informed about its background of translation and revision of translation. Do not neglect opportunity to call attention to the enormous amount of scholarship devoted to preserving, copying, and translating the Scriptures. We are not only indebted beyond measure to the "holy men of old" who wrote it under the direction of the Holy Spirit, but also to the great cloud of witnesses through whom it has come unaltered and undiluted to us.

Suggested further reading:

Buttrick, George Arthur. (ed.). *The Interpreter's Bible*. Nashville: Abingdon Press, 1952, I, 32–105.

McKnight, Edgar V. *Opening the Bible*. Nashville: Broadman Press, 1967, pp. 72–108.

Thomas, D. Winton, *et al. The Bible Today*. New York: Harper & Row, 1955.

Chapter 10

This concluding chapter was written in the hope of relating the message of the Bible to our contemporary Christian life, not in the sense of suggesting a Bible verse for every problem that arises, but as having to do with the very core of our nature as human beings. Consider with your class this question and their answers: What is the basic need of man? It is redemption, and that is the unifying and central theme of the Bible—the thread of redemption runs throughout it. What is man's relational need? It is community, and that is the meaning of church. But the church is not a "good fellowship club." It is a called (elected) remnant, having certain marks and living by the doing of certain things. Seek to use this concluding session to lead students to a more significant understanding of the church.

The Bible speaks to our day not only by pointing these things out to us as if they were historical realities, it speaks to us by helping us to experience these realities as present and personal. It not only tells us of redemption, it leads us to be redeemed. It not only reports that there is a community of redemption called church, it introduces us to it.

Suggested further reading:

Newbigin, Lesslie. *The Household of God.* New York: Friendship Press, 1954, pp. 26–122.

Nygren, Anders. *The Significance of the Bible for the Church.* Philadelphia: Fortress Press, 1963.

Rowley, H. H. *The Unity of the Bible.* Philadelphia: The Westminster Press, 1955.

Suggested Audiovisual Materials

Chapter 1
FILMSTRIPS: *God's Covenant with Israel,* 40 frames, color, recording; *Book of Books,* 44 frames, color, recording; *A Survey of the Bible,* 40 frames, color, recording

Chapter 2
FILMSTRIP: *What Baptists Believe About the Bible,* 50 frames, color, recording

Chapter 3
FILMSTRIPS: *The Wisdom of Egypt,* 42 frames, color, recording; *Egypt and the Bible,* 43 frames, color, recording; *God's Covenant with Israel,* 40 frames, color, recording; *The Pentateuch,* 42 frames, recording

Chapter 4
FILMSTRIPS: *The Rise of the Hebrew Nation,* 40 frames, color, recording; *The Decline of the Hebrew Nation,* 42 frames, color, recording; *God Keeps Covenant with His People,* 42 frames, color, recording

Chapter 5
FILMSTRIPS: *Making the Old Testament,* 41 frames, color, recording;

The Prophetical Books, 49 frames, color, recording; *The Books of Poetry,* 42 frames, color, recording

Chapter 6

FILMSTRIPS: *Between the Testaments,* 38 frames, color, recording; *Palestine in Jesus' Day,* Part I, 64 frames, color; *Palestine in Jesus' Day,* Part II, 60 frames, color; *The Land Where Jesus Lived,* 40 frames, color, recording; *John's Portrait of Jesus,* 50 frames, recording; *God's Covenant Fulfilled in Jesus Christ,* 43 frames, color, recording

MOTION PICTURE: *The Synagogue,* 22 minutes

Chapter 7

FILMSTRIPS: *The Book of Acts,* 41 frames, color, recording; *What Baptists Believe About the Church,* 50 frames, color, recording; *The Early Church—God's New Covenant People,* 40 frames, color, recording

Chapter 8

FILMSTRIPS: *The Four Gospels,* 37 frames, color, recording; *Making the New Testament,* 43 frames, color, recording; *Romans to Revelation,* 45 frames, color, recording

Chapter 9

FILMSTRIPS: *How We Got Our Bible,* set of four filmstrips, color, two recordings; *How Our Bible Came to Us,* set of four filmstrips, two recordings

MOTION PICTURES: "Our Bible: How It Came to Us"—Part I: *Formation of the Bible,* 25 minutes; Part II: *The Bible Crosses Europe,* 24 minutes; Part III: *Making of the English Bible,* 35 minutes

Chapter 10

FILMSTRIPS: *Book of Books,* 44 frames, color, recording; *The Early Church—God's New Covenant People,* 40 frames, color, recording

INSTRUCTIONS: If requested by the teacher, fill in this form and give it to him when the course is completed. If preferred, mail this request for course credit to

AWARDS OFFICE
THE SUNDAY SCHOOL BOARD, SBC
127 NINTH AVENUE, NORTH
NASHVILLE, TENNESSEE 37234

State Convention	Association	Indicate Type of Study (X)		Educational
		☐ Class ☐ Individual	☐ Lesson Course	☐ Institution

CHURCH

Church Name

Mailing Address

City, State, Zip Code

MAIL TO

Mail to (If Different from Church Address)

Street, Route, or P.O. Box

City, State, Zip Code

LAST NAME	FIRST NAME AND MIDDLE INITIAL	MRS. (X)	COURSE TITLE
			An Introduction to the Bible